WHOLE WORLD
C·O·O·K·B·O·O·K

D1124902

INTERNATIONAL MACROBIOTIC CUISINE

WHOLE WORLD
C·O·O·K·B·O·O·K

FROM THE EDITORS OF *EAST WEST JOURNAL*

AVERY PUBLISHING GROUP INC.
Wayne, New Jersey

AVERY PUBLISHING GROUP, INC.
89 Baldwin Terrace
Wayne, New Jersey 07470

ISBN 0-89529-231-9

Published in the United States of America

9 8 7 6 5 4 3 2

Designed by LM Sandhaus Madnick
Cover illustration by LM Sandhaus Madnick
Text illustrations by Melissa Sweet
Design Assistant Deborah Bowman

T·A·B·L·E O·F C·O·N·T·E·N·T·S

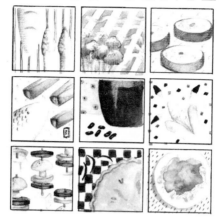

This book is dedicated to Georges Ohsawa and Michio Kushi, without whom the modern conception of international cuisine would be a "Big Mac."

On my way to Amsterdam in October, 1983 I visited Copenhagen; it was my first time in a Scandinavian country. I very much enjoyed this beautiful city—the lovely old buildings and parks reminded me of Hans Christian Andersen tales. Also in Copenhagen many wonderful organically-grown vegetables were available for use in my cooking classes.

In those cities I tasted herring for the first time. In Copenhagen it was simply salted and broiled, in Amsterdam it was their famous pickled herring. Even though I had been to Amsterdam many times before, that food had never been attractive to me. This time I discovered in its refreshing sea taste how appropriate a dish it is for that part of the world—the northern end of the Northern Hemisphere. My visits to Garmisch, Florence, Lisbon, and many other places have also shown me clearly how climate and environment influence people's traditional cooking to be in perfect balance with their locality.

Macrobiotic principles apply very well to the methods of traditional food selection and preparation. People in all parts of the world can return from chemicalized, artificially-processed foods to their original healthy, well-balanced diets. The modern communication and transportation systems now make it possible for East and West, North and South, to exchange ideas of healthy cooking.

The Whole World Cookbook can serve as a step in that direction, and can give you ideas for more variety in your own home cooking. By learning these different styles and recipes and matching them with your native land, you can understand the underlying sense of balance that influenced the development of traditional diets.

I appreciate the efforts of the contributing cooks and the *East West Journal* staff's work in finalizing this book.

Thank you.

Aveline Kushi
December 5, 1983
Brookline, Massachusetts

As a pioneer magazine in the natural lifestyle field, *East West Journal* has been emphasizing the idea of using everyday foods as a way to reestablish and maintain health. With the developments of modern medicine and food technology, many people have lost sight of the fact that our daily meals are the basis of our health and vitality. Yet this simple and sensible understanding underlies the teachings of Hippocrates (the father of modern medicine) and the traditional healers of the Orient. The importance of diet to health is as true now as it was thousands of years ago.

During the past thirteen years, the *Journal* has published over 150 cooking columns based on the premise that this age-old wisdom should not be forgotten. Each column has utilized only whole, natural, and unprocessed foods. Meals revolve around tasty and nutritious recipes that integrate the wholesomeness of hearty peasant-style eating with the requirements of modern nutrition. Having received many encouraging comments and letters from our readers over the years, including many requests for a single source of all the recipes, we have decided to publish *The Whole World Cookbook.*

This cookbook is a synthesis of the most festive recipes that have appeared in *East West Journal.*

It is oriented toward celebrations, not medicinal treatments, because we have seen that there is a need to present the best of natural foods cooking in a way that will encourage the use of whole foods by healthy people. For this reason, we have chosen some of the more elaborate of our past recipes. Many of these are not intended for daily use, but are meant for parties and special occasions where they may be shared with people who are unfamiliar with the natural foods.

Other plainer and simpler, but nonetheless delicious, recipes are suitable for daily consumption and for people seeking primarily to reestablish their health. Generally, the *Journal* has followed the macrobiotic style of natural foods cooking, wherein herbs, spices, eggs, and tomatoes are not recommended for use in daily fare. These ingredients generally should not be used at all by people following a restrictive type of diet. Simply stated, macrobiotics is a system of food preparation that encourages the use of whole, unprocessed foods, emphasizing whole cereal grains and fresh vegetables. Although we have not emphasized the more basic types of macrobiotic meals in *The Whole World Cookbook,* we have included one chapter of recipes for those who are completely new to natural foods cooking. We hope you will find these simpler recipes appealing and that you will go on to include more natural foods in all your cooking.

The editors would like to thank those cooks and columnists who originally contributed the recipes that were the source and inspiration of this cookbook. Special thanks go to Kathleen Bellicchi, Annemarie Colbin, Wendy Esko, Mary Estella, Barbara Jacobs, Ron Lemire, Lynda Lemole, Jean Strong Hurlle, and Rebecca Theurer Wood. Lima Ohsawa and Aveline Kushi not only contributed recipes but also, through their teaching, inspired many people to create unique cooking styles.

Susan Stayman helped to initiate the cookbook project and implemented the typing of the original manuscript, which was one of the most difficult jobs of all. She supervised the testing of many of the recipes and also wrote a number of new ones to fill out specific meals. We also thank the staff members of *East West Journal* who were very helpful in testing and tasting the many trial dishes which eventually developed into the polished recipes of this book.

Leonard Jacobs

The fragrance of bread still warm from the oven, the comforting murmur of a simmering vegetable soup, the crunchy tang of freshly made dill pickles—all evoke our intimate relationship with food. Cooking and eating are essential to life, and it is the cook's privilege to transform the mound of flour, the bunch of carrots, and the half-peck of baby cucumbers into mouth-watering sustenance for family and friends. Throughout history this has been accomplished in simple yet satisfying ways: several slices of whole grain bread served with a hearty vegetable soup; a steaming bowl of rice topped with slices of pickle; or corn tortillas enfolding a spicy pinto bean purée.

These combinations have sustained countless generations. Yet the traditional feasts prepared for celebrations and special occasions have been replaced by a more exotic idea of international cuisine—the type of "dining out" cooking we look forward to with heightened gastronomic anticipation. If, however, we examine the traditional methods of festive cooking from around the world, we will find that regardless of the variety of ingredients an intuitive sense of balance ensured that even these meals would be healthy and nutritious. Traditional meals revolved around whole grains such as wheat, corn, millet, rice, barley, or oats. Supplemented with side dishes of fresh vegetables, beans, and occasional animal foods and fruits, grain dishes have served not only as regular daily fare, but also as the basis of the most extravagant holiday meals. Even today, holiday dishes include such grain specialties as sushi, lasagna, arepas, stuffed grape leaves, and sizzling fried rice. Relearning traditional styles of cooking, while relying on whole grains as a staple, can allow us to create meals which are healthful as well as exciting.

To live we must eat. To live in health we must eat intelligently. But the question is, by whose intelligence? All too often, our impulses are not the same as the intuition that led our ancestors to search for wild greens each spring. The advertising and packaging techniques of the modern food industry have confused us with a multitude of options—most of which contradict the commonsense, traditional way of eating. However, it is possible to rediscover the healthful and delicious recipes of our ancestors and at the same time prepare appealing meals that satisfy the requirements of modern nutrition. It is also possible to learn to prepare tasty and elegant gourmet meals free of empty calories and saturated fats.

This is the orientation of *The Whole World Cookbook* —the preparation of delightful meals with an international flair. The dishes in *The Whole World Cookbook* taste good and nourish the body and soul. They illustrate the principles of balance in the cooking of traditional peoples and the application of modern knowledge and common sense in adapting them.

This method of balancing meals around whole grains is also the orientation of the monthly cooking columns of *East West Journal*. We have selected some of the most original and appetizing recipes from these columns, the discoveries of imaginative cooks who have synthesized traditional food preparation with the ideas of macrobiotic and natural foods cooking. *The Whole World Cookbook* is a natural foods cookbook, but at the same time it is an introduction to festive international cooking using the best of natural ingredients. Those of us who love to eat can be

certain that our meals will be enjoyable, wholesome, and nurturing. Those who love to cook will find menus and recipes that are fun to prepare and which make the experience of cooking rewarding and creative.

The study of nutrition concerns itself with food elements that are necessary for the body's building, maintenance, and energy. The cook's first and foremost responsibility is to present these essential nutrients so that the body can absorb them efficiently. Meals that use the finest ingredients, look inviting, and taste delicious reflect a job well done. The recipes in this book spring from this awareness. In addition, they are rooted in the ethnic charm and great cultural heritage of traditional peasant cooking which is, after all, the original natural foods cuisine— macrobiotics in its most fundamental sense.

Macrobiotics provides a sense of traditional wisdom in the area of food selection and balance to present meals which are, ultimately, the best in taste and healthfulness. The macrobiotic way of cooking considers the balancing of nutrients as equal in importance to the balancing of flavors, colors, and textures. The macrobiotic approach embraces traditional foods and cooking styles from around the world and unifies them in a cuisine which is extremely healthy and sound. In addition, macrobiotic meals can help you to establish a sense of balance with your environment, climate, and geographical location. Local foods can be substituted for the listed ingredients in order to make each meal completely suitable for wherever you live. Although these recipes utilize ingredients such as tamari soy sauce, tofu, tempeh, seitan, kuzu, and agar, which may seem exotic at first, these ingredients are not complicated to use and will soon become familiar substances in your kitchen. Let *The Whole World Cookbook* be your guide.

The Whole World Cookbook will give you menus and recipes, but we hope above all that it will act as a springboard for your own creativity. These recipes are just a beginning—we hope you will expand upon them according to your nature, judgment, and desire, and adapt them to your personal heritage and needs. Recipe is not an English word, but a Latin imperative meaning "procure." So "recipe" the best of ingredients— as fresh as can be found, and preserve their identity in preparation.

We encourage you to use sensitivity in your cooking, to develop your own unique recipes that will be requested and shared many times over. Cooking has always been an oral tradition, passed down from parent to child, from master to apprentice. It is not a mystery. The way to be a cook is to cook. We sincerely hope that this book will encourage and inspire you to do just that.

The Editors

F·R·E·N·C·H

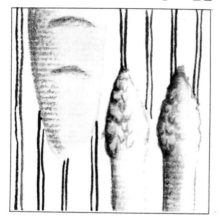

Stuffed Mushroom Caps
Rich Onion Soup with Herbed Croutons
Poisson en Croûte with Béchamel Sauce
Herbed Rice
Carrots Vichy
Steamed Asparagus
Salade Jeannette
French Bread
Coffee Mousse

French cooks have always understood the importance of serving a meal that will not only fill empty stomachs but also delight the eye and appeal to the taste buds. A well-prepared and beautifully served meal lets the cares of the day be forgotten. The participants leave refreshed, the meal now another warm memory, perhaps to be celebrated in the future by an aspiring Proust.

The fabled *haute cuisine* is a rich and heavy culinary tradition, employing large amounts of cream, butter, eggs, pork, and well-marbled beef. Currently, however, French cooking is undergoing a metamorphosis. Just as Japanese painting and colorful, stylized woodblock prints influenced nineteenth -century French Impressionist painters, the influence of Japanese culinary arts is being felt in today's classic French cooking. Along with nutritional and health concerns, a Japanese influence is discernible in the much lighter and more refreshing *nouvelle cuisine*. Characterized by the use of fewer dairy products and meats and the inclusion of more fish and fresh vegetables, *nouvelle cuisine* is still distinctively French.

The traditional French emphases on the freshest of ingredients and the use of perfect sauces, as well as the principles of *nouvelle cuisine,* lend themselves well to macrobiotic cooking for those very special occasions.

Menu (Serves 6-8)
Stuffed Mushroom Caps
French Bread
Rich Onion Soup with Herbed
   Croutons
Salade Jeannette
Poisson en Croûte with Béchamel
   Sauce
Herbed Rice
Carrots Vichy
Steamed Asparagus
Coffee Mousse

Cooking Suggestions
■ French Bread and Coffee Mousse can be made ahead of time, the bread stored at room temperature and the mousse kept chilled. Mushroom Caps can be stuffed in advance, stored in the refrigerator, and baked just before serving. Carrots Vichy and Steamed Asparagus should be made at the last minute.

Stuffed Mushroom Caps

16 MEDIUM-SIZED FRESH MUSHROOMS

½ CUP ARAME

1 ONION

1 TABLESPOON SESAME OIL

¼ CUP SAKE

2 TABLESPOONS TAMARI

1 LEMON, JUICED

Rinse mushrooms and remove stems. Dice stems and set aside.

Rinse arame to remove any sand and grit. Drain, cover with water, and soak for 10 minutes. Drain off soaking water and place arame in a saucepan with enough water to half cover. Bring to a boil and simmer for 15 minutes. Cool, squeeze out liquid, and chop finely.

Mince onion. Heat oil in a pan and sauté onion and mushroom stems over medium flame for 2-3 minutes. Add arame and continue to sauté.

Combine sake, tamari, and lemon juice. Pour half this liquid over arame mixture and simmer until liquid evaporates.

Place mushroom caps round sides down on a baking dish. Pour remaining marinade over mushroom caps, fill with arame mixture, and bake at 350° F. for 20 minutes, or until browned.

French Bread   2 loaves

2 TABLESPOONS DRY YEAST

2 ½ CUPS WARM WATER

3 CUPS WHOLE WHEAT FLOUR

3 CUPS UNBLEACHED WHITE FLOUR

½ TEASPOON SEA SALT

In a large mixing bowl, dissolve yeast in warm water. Sift the two flours together. Add 2 cups flour and the ½ teaspoon salt to the yeast, and beat for 2 minutes with a wire whisk. Add remaining flour and mix with a wooden spoon to form dough.

Begin kneading lightly on a floured surface. Knead for 5 minutes and form into a ball. Place ball of dough in an oiled bowl and turn over once. Let it rise in a warm and humid area, covered with a damp towel, until doubled in size (about 45 minutes). Punch down and let rise again until doubled in size (about 30-40 minutes more). Punch down again, and let dough sit for 5 minutes or so.

Divide dough in half, roll out one half to an 8″ x 12″ rectangle and fold in thirds. Roll (to an 8″ x 12″ rectangle) and fold twice more, then form into a lengthwise cylinder. Brush bottom of loaf on board to smooth seam. Repeat with the other half of the dough. Place cylinders on a cookie sheet that has been sprinkled lightly with corn-meal. Cover, and let rise until dough is springy to the touch (about 40-60 minutes). Place in a preheated, 400° F. oven and bake for 15 minutes. Turn oven down to 350° F. for 30 minutes more, brushing bread with water occasionally to form crust, or until bread sounds hollow when tapped.

Rich Onion Soup

1 STRIP KOMBU, 3 INCHES LONG

5 CUPS WATER

5 ONIONS

½ TEASPOON SEA SALT (OR TO TASTE)

3-4 TABLESPOONS TAMARI (OR TO TASTE)

Wipe kombu with a clean cloth to remove any dust. Place in a soup pot with 5 cups of water, bring to a boil, lower flame, and simmer for 10-20 minutes. Remove kombu and reserve for use in another dish, and set kombu stock aside.

Slice onions lengthwise, then turn each half flat side down and slice very thin. Place onions in a saucepan so that it is three-quarters filled. Stir constantly over medium heat until onions are warm through. Add salt and continue to stir until onions go limp and their juice has been released (about 15 minutes). Season with tamari and cook for 5 more minutes.

Add kombu stock, cover, and simmer soup for 20 minutes. Top each bowl with herbed croutons and garnish with thinly sliced scallions.

Herbed Croutons

3 SLICES WHOLE WHEAT SOURDOUGH BREAD, ½" THICK (See Transitional Section)

1 ½ TABLESPOONS CORN OR SESAME OIL

1 TABLESPOON TAMARI OR SHOYU

⅛-¼ TEASPOON EACH OREGANO, SAGE, THYME

1 CLOVE GARLIC, MINCED

Cut bread into ½" cubes. Combine oil, tamari, herbs, and garlic in mixing bowl. Toss bread cubes in mixture to coat well. Spread on baking sheet and bake in 350°F. oven for 20 minutes or until crisp.

Salade Jeannette

1 BUNCH WATERCRESS

½ LARGE HEAD CAULIFLOWER

1 POUND GREEN BEANS

3 TABLESPOONS OLIVE OIL

1 TABLESPOON RICE VINEGAR

4 TABLESPOONS FRESH LEMON JUICE

2 TEASPOONS DIJON MUSTARD (OPTIONAL)

¼ TEASPOON SEA SALT

1 SHALLOT, CUT INTO SEVERAL PIECES

¼ CUP FINELY CHOPPED PARSLEY

Wash the watercress under cold water, and cut into 1 ½" pieces. Place in a glass bowl or on a serving platter. Separate the cauliflower into flowerets and steam until just tender (about 4 minutes). Snap tops off beans and steam until tender (about 4 minutes). Leave the beans whole or French them by cutting into long thin slices. Cool cauliflower and beans and add them to the watercress.

Combine oil, rice vinegar, lemon juice, mustard, salt, and shallot in a blender or a suribachi. Blend until smooth and creamy. Pour over vegetables and toss lightly.

Poisson en Croûte

This entree consists of layers of grain, greens, and fish wrapped in a tender crust and topped with béchamel sauce. Tofu may be substituted for fish with excellent results if slight adjustments are made in preparing the crust and sauce. Complete directions for both variations are included below.

1. PREPARATION
Pastry Dough

3 CUPS PASTRY FLOUR OR 2 CUPS PASTRY AND 1 CUP CORN FLOUR

½ CUP CORN OIL

1 CUP WATER

½ TEASPOON SEA SALT

Rub oil into flour with hands to the consistency of cornmeal. Bring water and salt to a boil, pour over flour, and stir until dough forms a ball. Knead lightly 10 times. Divide dough in half and chill 1 hour.

Fish

1 ½ POUNDS WHITE FISH, ½″ THICK FILLETS

Wash fish and trim if necessary. Set aside.

For Tofu en Croûte:

½ POUND TOFU

1 CUP WATER

¼ CUP TAMARI OR SHOYU

½ TEASPOON MUSTARD

½ TEASPOON DRIED HORSERADISH (WASABI) POWDER

Slice tofu lengthwise into 4 strips ½″ thick. Marinate for 1 hour in 1 cup of water seasoned with tamari or shoyu, mustard, and wasabi.

Stuffing

2 CUPS WATER
1 TEASPOON TAMARI
½-1 TEASPOON SAFFRON
1 CUP UNCOOKED COUSCOUS
½ POUND SPINACH OR PARSLEY

Bring water, tamari, and saffron to a boil. Simmer gently for about 5 minutes, until the liquid is light orange. Pour over couscous and let sit until liquid is absorbed.

Wash and drain spinach. Remove stems. Blanch by dropping into salted boiling water for 15 to 30 seconds, then chop finely. (Parsley, if chopped, doesn't need to be blanched.)

Béchamel Sauce

1 TABLESPOON SESAME OIL
1 TABLESPOON UNBLEACHED WHITE FLOUR
1 CUP LUKEWARM WATER
½ TEASPOON SEA SALT
½ TEASPOON GRATED FRESH GINGER ROOT (omit if you are preparing Tofu en Croûte)

Heat oil in saucepan over medium-low flame. Add flour, stirring to prevent scorching. When this mixture (the roux) is slightly golden, whisk in water and stir for a few minutes until thickened. Add salt and ginger, and cook for 1 more minute.

This is a quick-to-prepare, all-purpose sauce, similar to the familiar white sauce of conventional cooking. Add seasonings toward the end of cooking to complement the dish the sauce will be served over—nutmeg or coriander is very good with vegetables, for example. Make a béchamel without seasoning if you just want to add extra richness to already flavorful dishes.

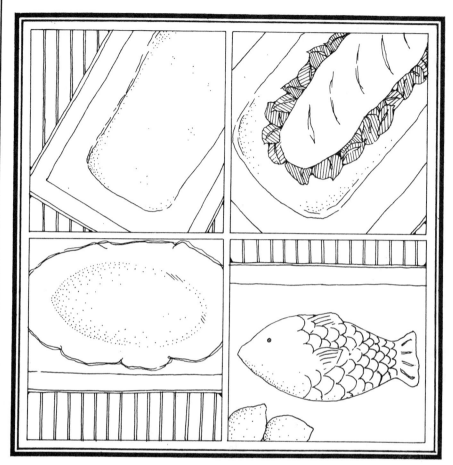

Assembly of Poisson en Croûte as explained on page 10. With imagination and simple kitchen tools a handsome "fish" can be created.

2. ASSEMBLY

Shape 1 ball of dough into a log and roll out, between two pieces of waxed paper or on a lightly floured surface, to a 12" x 6" rectangle, ¼" thick. Transfer onto a lightly oiled baking sheet. Spread couscous ½" thick down the center of the dough, the same length and width as fish fillets. Spread spinach or parsley over couscous. Lay fillets on greens and top with half the béchamel sauce. Bring dough up around fillets on 3 sides, shaping the fourth end like a fishtail. If you substitute tofu for fish, place tofu slices end to end on top of the greens and omit fishtail shape.

Roll out second ball of dough the same as the first. Place this dough so it covers the entire "fish" or loaf and hangs down to touch the baking sheet. Trim away any excess and tuck dough under on 3 sides to seal. Shape fourth side into tail for "fish." Prick fork holes around on all sides of dough to allow steam to escape and to prevent the crust from splitting. Imprint "scales" on top of the fish with a melonballer or spoon. Press through the dough in a few places to allow more steam to escape.

For Tofu en Croûte, seal the loaf all around. Cut diagonal slits in the top crust to mark portions and allow steam to escape.

Bake in a preheated 350° F. oven for 20-30 minutes. Check after 20 minutes and remove when crust is golden and sounds hollow when tapped. Transfer to a serving platter, cover with remaining sauce, and garnish with lemon slices and parsley sprigs.

Herbed Rice

2 TABLESPOONS SESAME OIL
2 ONIONS, CHOPPED
2 CLOVES GARLIC, PRESSED
1 TABLESPOON FRESH PARSLEY, MINCED
¼ TEASPOON EACH, SLIGHTLY CRUSHED, MARJORAM, CHERVIL, SAVORY, AND THYME
3 CUPS COOKED BROWN RICE (see page 107)

Heat a skillet or wok and add oil. Lightly brown onions, adding garlic when onions are transparent. Add herbs and rice, cover, and cook for 8 minutes, stirring occasionally.

Carrots Vichy

| 2 POUNDS WHOLE BABY CARROTS |
| 2 CUPS VICHY OR OTHER NON-SPARKLING MINERAL WATER |
| SEA SALT |
| 1 TABLESPOON ARROWROOT POWDER |
| 1 TEASPOON MINCED WATERCRESS OR PARSLEY |

Wash carrots. Use baby carrots whole; slice regular carrots into ¼″ rounds. Place carrots in a saucepan, cover with mineral water, add a pinch of salt, and bring gently to simmer. Cover pot to seal in flavor and allow to cook slowly for 30-45 minutes, reducing liquid until about ¼ cup remains.

When carrots are soft and tender, remove them from pan, reserving the cooking water. Dissolve arrowroot in one-quarter cup of cool water and add to liquid remaining in pan. Stir and simmer sauce for 2-3 minutes, until it is clear and shiny.

Either return carrots to glaze and mix, or pour glaze over carrots in serving dish. Garnish with watercress or parsley.

Steamed Asparagus

| 1 POUND ASPARAGUS |
| 2 TABLESPOONS WHITE MISO |
| 1 TEASPOON LEMON JUICE |

Wash asparagus and gently bend bottom ends of stalks until stringy or woody parts break off. Place asparagus in a steamer over boiling water and cook for 5 minutes. Soften miso in 4 tablespoons water and heat in a skillet, adding asparagus and cooking for 4-5 minutes. Transfer to a serving dish and sprinkle lemon juice over it.

Coffee Mousse

1 QUART APPLE JUICE

5 TABLESPOONS AGAR FLAKES

1 TABLESPOON DRY INSTANT GRAIN COFFEE

PINCH OF SEA SALT

2 TABLESPOONS TAHINI

1 TEASPOON VANILLA EXTRACT

1 TABLESPOON BARLEY MALT

SEVERAL WALNUTS, SHELLED

Place apple juice in a saucepan over medium heat and sprinkle in agar flakes, stirring with a wire whisk. Turn up heat and bring liquid to a boil. Reduce heat and simmer for 15 minutes, stirring constantly. Dilute grain coffee in a little cool apple juice. Add diluted coffee and salt, remove from heat, and let cool until set.

When mixture has jelled, put it in a blender along with tahini, vanilla, and barley malt. Blend briefly until smooth. Pour into wine glasses and chill. Toast walnuts in 350° F. oven 10-15 minutes or until fragrant, then chop. Decorate mousse with walnuts just before serving.

Variations
■ For a light supper make only Rich Onion Soup, French Bread, and Salade Jeannette.
■ For a special luncheon party serve Stuffed Mushrooms, Poisson en Croûte with Béchamel Sauce, Herbed Rice, Steamed Asparagus, and Coffee Mousse.
■ Leftover Rich Onion Soup can be simmered for several hours until very thick to make a tasty spread for French Bread.

I·T·A·L·I·A·N

Antipasto
Florentine White Bean Soup
Pasta with Estella's Red Sauce
and "Mozzarella Cheese"
Stewed Broccoli Rabe
Garlic Bread
Insalata Verde
Cherry-Almond Gelée

The story has it that when Dwight Eisenhower was in Italy in the early '50s he became enamored of an Italian dish. A rather messy affair, the dish consisted of bread or a kind of pie dough covered with stewed vegetables. At home in the White House, Ike and his chef worked out the recipe as best they could. They finally came up with a flat, round crust covered with stewed herbed tomatoes and bits of Ike's favorite vegetables and meats, topped with mounds of grated cheese which, they discovered, melted sensuously when the entire mixture was baked. Soon "pizza" parlors popped up all around the country and the U.S. had acquired a new national treasure. Unfortunately this craze spread most rapidly along with the decline in the quality of the ingredients. The current conception of pizza is far from the original hearty vegetable/bread combination that sustained generations of Southern Italians. Now it is little more than saturated fat, sodium, and calories served over a crust of bleached white flour and sugar.

To most Americans, tomato sauce is the foundation of Italian cooking. And indeed it does play a starring role in the cooking of Southern Italy. The tomato, however, wasn't used with regularity in Italy until the 19th century—two hundred years after its introduction to Italy from South America. Up until this time Europeans considered it to be poisonous. In Italy today many wonderful dishes are being served that contain nary a speck of red. In fact, the cooking of northern Italy is close to Swiss and French cooking and rarely, if ever, contains tomatoes. For a special treat, and for inspiration in your own cooking, try to find Italian cookbooks or restaurants that specialize in the cuisine of the northern regions.

Since the tomato is an extremely acidic food, and one not regularly included in a macrobiotic diet, we present here an unusual non-tomato "tomato sauce" which can be used as often as you like.

What actually gives Italian cuisine its distinctive flavor is the use of oregano, basil, and garlic. Adventurous natural foods cooks will find these herbs perfect enhancements to a wide range of festive grain, vegetable, and bean dishes—just as Italian cooks have for generations.

Menu (Serves 6-8)

Antipasto
Florentine White Bean Soup
Pasta with Estella's Red Sauce
    and "Mozzarella Cheese"
Stewed Broccoli Rabe
Garlic Bread
Insalata Verde with
    Lemon Dressing
Cherry-Almond Gelée

Cooking Suggestions

■ For best results, make the spaghetti sauce and the "Mozzarella cheese" the day before. This allows the flavors in the sauce to blend and the "cheese" to ripen. The Antipasto also can be made ahead of time, and stored in the refrigerator until ready to serve.

■ Since the beans for the soup need to soak for several hours, you may find it convenient to soak them overnight.

Antipasto

Antipasto ("before pasta") is the first course of an Italian meal. A traditional antipasto would include a sampling of salty cheeses, olives, sausages, and marinated mushrooms and peppers, meant to be leisurely eaten with bread and wine. An adapted antipasto may include tofu or tempeh cubes (either fried or marinated), leftover cooked grain formed into little balls and rolled in seeds or deep-fried, and garlicky miso-tahini spread served with crackers or celery. The antipasto tray may be garnished with parsley, toasted nori strips, radishes, olives, and pickles. With such additions, this platter can be transformed from a first course to a party platter or even into a main course.

Florentine White Bean Soup

1 CUP DRY NAVY BEANS

1 STRIP KOMBU, 2 INCHES LONG

8 OUNCES SPINACH NOODLES (FETTUCCINE OR ELBOW)

1 CARROT

1 ONION

1 GREEN PEPPER

1 SMALL ZUCCHINI

PINCH OF OREGANO, BASIL, OR OTHER HERBS

2-3 TEASPOONS WHITE MISO DISSOLVED IN ¼ CUP WATER

1 CUP FRESH GREENS (COLLARD GREENS, BEET GREENS, WATERCRESS), STEAMED LIGHTLY AND CHOPPED

Soak beans for several hours together with kombu in water to cover. Pressure cook for 45 minutes or boil until beans are tender. Boil noodles al dente, then drain and rinse them under cold water. Slice carrot into matchsticks, dice onion and pepper, and slice zucchini into half moons. Layer vegetables, except greens, in a large soup pot. Gently add water to cover and simmer for 10 minutes. Add beans and kombu, noodles, oregano, and miso. Add more water if you want a thinner soup. Simmer for 10 more minutes. Just before serving, add chopped greens.

Pasta with Red Sauce and "Mozzarella Cheese"

1. PREPARATION
Estella's Red Sauce

1 POUND CARROTS

1 SMALL BEET (FOR COLOR)

2 ONIONS

BAY LEAF

1-2 TABLESPOONS RED OR KOME MISO, DISSOLVED IN 2 CUPS WATER

2 CLOVES GARLIC

¼ TEASPOON BASIL

¼ TEASPOON OREGANO

2 TABLESPOONS ARROWROOT, DISSOLVED IN ¼ CUP COOL WATER

Scrub carrots and beet and cut them into 1″ cubes. Place carrots, then beets in a pressure cooker or heavy soup pot with lid. Peel and dice onions and add them to carrots and beets. Add bay leaf and dissolved miso to vegetables. If pressure cooking, add 1 inch more of water, cover, and pressure cook for 15 minutes. If using soup pot, add water to cover vegetables and boil in covered pot for 1 hour or until vegetables are very tender. Season with garlic, basil, and oregano. (Garlic can be sautéed first in olive oil for extra flavor.)

Purée vegetables in a food mill or blender, adding vegetable cooking water as needed. Return to pressure cooker or soup pot and heat uncovered. Add arrowroot for a thicker texture. Simmer 5-10 minutes, stirring until smooth.

This sauce is delicious on pizza, ravioli, and lasagna, as well as on spaghetti.

"Mozzarella Cheese"

1 CUP SWEET RICE
1-1½ CUPS WATER
1 ONION
1 TEASPOON CORN OIL
16 OUNCES TOFU
1 TEASPOON UMEBOSHI PASTE
PINCH SEA SALT
1 TABLESPOON TAHINI

Wash and drain 1 cup sweet rice (see Glossary) and place in pressure cooker with 1 cup water. Bring up to pressure, reduce heat to low, and cook for 40 minutes. Let pressure come down and remove sweet rice to a wooden bowl. (For boiling, increase water to 1 ½ cups and cover tightly. Bring to boil, reduce heat to low, and cook for 50-60 minutes.) Pound sweet rice with a wooden pestle till most of the grains are mashed and the substance is very sticky.

Mince onion and sauté in oil. Add tofu, minced onion, umeboshi paste, salt, and tahini to the sweet rice and continue pounding until well blended. Let this ripen for a day or two at room temperature. This makes 2 cups of thick, chewy, cheese-like topping which can be used in a variety of ways depending on your creativity.

2. ASSEMBLY

Cook 16 ounces whole wheat spaghetti or other pasta (see page 114) al dente, drain, and rinse immediately under cold water.

Place pasta in baking dish, pour sauce over, and cover with "cheese." Bake in preheated 350° F. oven for 10 minutes or until "cheese" begins to bubble.

Stewed Broccoli Rabe

2 BUNCHES BROCCOLI RABE (OR DANDELION OR MUSTARD GREENS)

2 LARGE ONIONS

2 CLOVES GARLIC

2 FRESH TOMATOES (Optional)

1 TEASPOON OLIVE OIL (Optional)

1 TABLESPOON TAMARI

Wash greens carefully and chop into 1″ pieces. Slice onions and mince garlic. Chop tomatoes. Pour 2″ water into a heavy pot and layer greens, onions, tomatoes, and garlic. Top with oil and tamari. Place a heat-resistant plate or a lid that fits inside the pot directly on the contents, and then cover. Cook over medium heat until bubbling, then lower heat to simmer and cook 20-30 minutes. Serve in the liquid.

Garlic Bread

1 LOAF FRENCH OR ITALIAN-STYLE BREAD (See French Dinner for bread recipe)

3 TABLESPOONS CORN OIL

2 LARGE CLOVES FRESH GARLIC, SQUEEZED THROUGH GARLIC PRESS

2 TABLESPOONS CHOPPED FRESH PARSLEY

Cut bread into 1-inch slices and lay flat on a baking sheet. Mix oil and garlic juice together and brush about half of this mixture onto bread. Sprinkle with parsley flakes and broil until golden. Then turn bread, coat other side, sprinkle with parsley, and again broil until golden.

Insalata Verde

Use various leafy greens, including lettuce, watercress, escarole, chicory, and others in season. Wash greens carefully. Either chop them or leave them whole, and toss with dressing.

Lemon Dressing

| 2 UMEBOSHI PLUMS, PITTED, OR 1 TABLESPOON UMEBOSHI PASTE |
| 1 TEASPOON FRESH LEMON JUICE |
| ½ CUP WATER |

Blend all ingredients in a suribachi.

Cherry-Almond Gelée

| 6 CUPS APPLE-CHERRY JUICE OR APPLE JUICE |
| 5 TABLESPOONS AGAR FLAKES |
| ¼ TEASPOON SEA SALT |
| 2 CUPS PITTED CHERRIES |
| 1 TABLESPOON KUZU POWDER, THOROUGHLY DISSOLVED IN ¼ CUP COOL WATER |
| ¾ CUP SHELLED ALMONDS |

Whisk agar flakes into juice and bring to a boil. Add salt and cherries and simmer for 10 minutes. Add dissolved kuzu to juice mixture and stir over medium heat until it begins to thicken. Pour into a dish which has been rinsed with cold water.

Toast almonds in 375° F. oven till fragrant and slice fine while still warm. Sprinkle almonds on gelée and let sit until jelled.

Variations

■ For casual family meals with a special touch, try these combinations: spaghetti with Estella's Red Sauce, and Insalata; White Bean Soup, Insalata, and Cherry-Almond Gelée.

■ For picnics, make Antipasto and Garlic Bread. Take along a bottle of wine if you like.

■ Melt leftover "Mozzarella Cheese" on leftover Garlic Bread and tuck it into lunchboxes for an unexpected treat. Send along simple accompaniments like carrot and celery sticks and applesauce.

J·A·P·A·N·E·S·E

Norimaki Sushi
Udon Doughnuts in Vegetable Soup
Sukiyaki
Mountain Soybeans
Boiled Watercress and
Mustard Greens
Quick Radish Pickles
Fruit Kanten

Our usual conception of Japanese cooking includes sushi, sashimi, tempura, and noodles. Yet this is actually only one type of Japanese meal—the one available in modern Japanese restaurants in America. Traditionally, the Japanese peasant meal has included an entire range of grain and vegetable dishes, with only occasional fish and other animal foods.

The meal presented here is more in keeping with the home-style Japanese meal that you would discover if you spent time touring Japan and dining at guest houses or country inns. Even the sushi is different from what you might expect—using unsugared, whole grain brown rice and fresh vegetables. In Japanese, "sushi" actually means "special," and can refer to any number of unique ways of presenting rice dishes. In this meal we have included a "norimaki" sushi, with nori sea vegetable wrapped around rice and vegetables.

Overall, the meal presented here is one that you can be certain is authentic, elegant, and healthful. It also includes traditional home-made pickles, which are eaten daily throughout Japan as an aid to digestion.

Menu (Serves 6-8)
Norimaki Sushi
Udon Doughnuts in Vegetable Soup
Sukiyaki
Mountain Soybeans
Boiled Watercress and
  Mustard Greens
Quick Radish Pickles
Fruit Kanten

Cooking Suggestions
■ Radish pickles can be prepared up to 1 week in advance. Norimaki Sushi, Mountain Soybeans, and Fruit Kanten can be made the day before. Vegetables for Sukiyaki can be cut and arranged in a skillet ahead of time. Beans for Mountain Soybeans need to be soaked for 12 to 18 hours.

Norimaki Sushi

Sushi is easy to prepare and adds a festive touch to daily meals as well as party buffets. Fillings can be simple or elaborate, hearty or light.

Traditionally, sushi is prepared by wrapping vinegared rice and vegetables in nori, or spreading fingers of rice with wasabi (Japanese horseradish) and topping with fish (usually raw) or vegetables. Either way, it is then served with a small dish of tamari soy sauce for dipping. However, vegetable-filled sushi can be prepared with umeboshi plums instead of vinegar.

2 SHEETS NORI

½ CARROT

1 SCALLION, GREENS ONLY

½ CUCUMBER, PEELED AND SEEDED

2 CUPS COOKED BROWN RICE (see page 107)

1 TABLESPOON UMEBOSHI PASTE

A bamboo sushi mat is needed for rolling sushi and can be readily obtained at an Oriental grocery or specialty store.

Toast nori by passing it over a gas flame (or medium heat on an electric stove) until the color changes from black or dark green to a brighter green.

Cut carrot into thin julienne strips and steam until just cooked (about 4-5 minutes). Also cut the scallions and cucumber julienne-style.

Position bamboo mat so that you can roll it away from you. Center one sheet of nori rough side up on mat. With wet hands place some rice on the center of the nori. Carefully spread rice and press down gently to ½" thickness, leaving a 1" extension of nori uncovered at end opposite from you.

Spread a dab of umeboshi paste across center of rice in a line from left to right. Place a few carrot, cucumber, and scallion strips in a thin layer on top of umeboshi.

To roll sushi, use your thumbs and carefully pick up the mat by the margin close to you. Reach over with fingertips to hold filling in place as you begin to roll. Gently but firmly push sushi mat away from you, keeping hold of mat end so that it doesn't roll into the sushi. Brush nori extension at opposite end with a little water to make it sticky. When roll lies over the extension, hold it there for a few seconds to allow nori to make a seal.

Remove sushi roll from mat to cutting board and slice with a sharp wet knife into about 8 equal pieces. Repeat rolling procedure with remaining ingredients.

Arrange sliced sushi flat on serving plate so the beautiful center filling can be seen, and garnish plate either with a sprig of parsley or water-cress or a flower such as chrysanthemum.

A sauce for dipping sushi at table can be made with equal parts shoyu and water and a few drops of juice from grated fresh ginger root. Serve sauce in small shallow ceramic containers next to each person's dinner plate.

☐ With a little practice sushi is easy and fairly quick to prepare. Use your imagination to create fillings, or try the following suggestions:

BEETS. Boil whole, drain well, cut in julienne-style pieces. Beets are beautiful with white rice, and their flavor enhances scallions or chard.

BURDOCK. Slice pre-cooked burdock thinly on diagonal and sauté lightly, seasoning with umeboshi or tamari and freshly grated ginger. Try burdock with a lightly vinegared rice, either alone or with minced parsley. (To make vinegared rice, add 1 teaspoon rice vinegar to each cup of cooked rice; stir in gently.) Burdock and slivered cucumber also make a good combination.

FISH. Raw fish, such as tuna, sole, or perch is a popular traditional Japanese filling. Wasabi should be used with raw fish instead of ume-boshi paste.

NOODLES. Use instead of rice. Spread 2/3 cup of cooked noodles crosswise on the nori and proceed as with rice sushi.

SCALLIONS. Slice in half lengthwise; use raw or blanch in boiling water. Use scallions alone or with other fillings.

Preparation of Norimaki Sushi as explained on page 26. After beginning to roll, be careful to keep mat from rolling into sushi.

STRING BEANS. Blanch and use whole. String beans are very tasty combined with scallions and tofu.

SWISS CHARD. Steam briefly to retain fresh green color. Remove stems and slice them in half. Cut greens in half or thirds lengthwise and trim ends to fit on rice. Try red or green chard with cucumber.

TAMARI/KOMBU. Soak small amount of kombu till soft, then simmer slowly in 3 parts water and 1 part tamari until most of the liquid has evaporated. Cut into thin strips. Kombu in sushi heightens the flavors of carrots and/or scallions.

TOFU. Slice tofu in thirds across the width of the cake. Cook in a lightly oiled skillet about 5 minutes, turn once, and season with tamari. Slice each piece of tofu into ½-inch strips. Tofu works well combined with almost any filling ingredients.

WATERCRESS. Blanch whole watercress sprigs and immerse in cold water immediately to retain a fresh green color. Trim sprigs slightly if necessary. Watercress is especially delicious combined with strips of omelet or tofu as cooked above.

Udon Doughnuts in Vegetable Soup

3 CUPS UNBLEACHED WHITE FLOUR
½ TEASPOON SEA SALT
WATER
ONE STRIP KOMBU, 4 INCHES LONG
2 DRIED SHIITAKE MUSHROOMS (SOAKED 7-10 MINUTES IN COOL WATER TO COVER)
6 CUPS WATER
¼ SMALL WINTER SQUASH OR PUMPKIN
½ SMALL CHINESE CABBAGE
1 TEASPOON SESAME OIL
5 SCALLIONS
½ SHEET NORI
½ BUNCH WATERCRESS

1 ½ TABLESPOONS TAMARI

Combine flour and salt in a large bowl. Add enough water, while slowly mixing, to form a soft pastry dough. Knead lightly with one hand, turning the dough in a spiral. To do this, pick up top right corner of dough and fold in toward the center, then press with your palm curving from the bottom right to the upper left. Lift your hand and grasp the new section at the top upper right again, etc.

Continue kneading until the surface becomes very smooth and has no lumps. Form dough into 1 ½″ balls and arrange on a tray. Cover with a thin damp cotton cloth and let sit 1-1 ½ hours.

For soup, wipe kombu strip and place in pot with shiitake mushrooms and the 6 cups of water. Bring to boil, then lower flame and simmer for 10 minutes. Heat another pan, brush with sesame oil, and sauté the winter squash and cabbage, both cut into 1″ squares, for about 2 minutes. Remove kombu and shiitake from soup stock and add cabbage, winter squash, and a pinch of salt. Bring to a boil, then simmer on low flame 15-20 minutes. While soup is simmering, chop scallions into small rounds, wrap in light cotton cloth, and rub while running under cold water for about 1 minute. This removes stickiness and makes the scallions crisper. Set them aside for garnish. Toast sheet of nori and slice once lengthwise down the middle. Place these two halves together and slice crosswise into 1″ strips. Stack these strips together and slice crosswise again so you end up with thin slivers 1″ long. Put these aside also for a garnish.

To make udon doughnuts, grasp opposite sides of each dough ball and stretch to about 4 inches. The shape should be wider at the ends and thinner in the middle. Then put your fingers into the thin middle area and pull apart, making a hole in the dough. Keep pulling gently until the dough makes a ring (it will not be a perfect shape). Drop rings into soup, add tamari and finely chopped watercress, and cook another 7 minutes or until rings float to top. Serve with scallion and nori garnish.

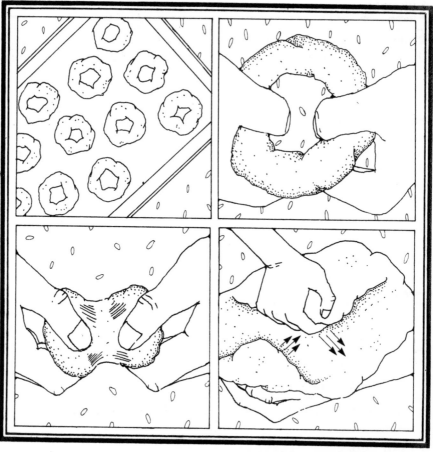

Preparation of Udon Doughnuts as explained on pages 29 and 30. "Doughnuts" will be about 2″ in diameter before cooking.

Sukiyaki

Sukiyaki is a one-dish meal, cooked in flavored broth and served in the same cast-iron skillet. It includes a variety of different vegetables, noodles, seitan (see page 110), and, optionally, fish—or any combination of these.

Sukiyaki can be cooked in plain water and then served at the table with dipping sauce (see Sushi, page 27). The diners pluck delicacies from the communal pot with chopsticks, dip them in sauce, and pop them into their mouths. Sukiyaki thus creates an ambiance of informality and intimacy.

1 MEDIUM ONION, QUARTERED OR CUT INTO ROUNDS
4-6 BROCCOLI FLOWERETS
1 LARGE CARROT, SLICED DIAGONALLY INTO CHUNKS
¼ HEAD CABBAGE, QUARTERED
5-6 LARGE SLICES BUTTERCUP SQUASH
5-6 FRESH MUSHROOMS
PINCH OF SEA SALT
$^1/_3$ CUP SAKE OR MIRIN
½ TEASPOON JUICE SQUEEZED FROM GRATED FRESH GINGER ROOT
2 TABLESPOONS TAMARI
½ CAKE TOFU, CUT INTO 1″ CUBES
1 BUNCH WATERCRESS, WHOLE SPRIGS

Place onion, broccoli, carrot chunks, cabbage, squash, and mushrooms in a skillet so that each vegetable has its own separate place and is not mixed with any others. Arrange vegetables so that the colors are balanced and attractive. Add enough water to cover bottom of skillet. Sprinkle with a pinch of salt. Cover skillet and bring to a boil. Reduce flame to low and simmer 10 minutes or until vegetables are tender. Combine sake, ginger juice, and tamari and pour into skillet. When mixture is simmering again, cover and cook 2-3 minutes. Add tofu, cover, and cook 2-3 minutes more. Add watercress, cover, and cook 1 more minute. Serve hot in the skillet.

Mountain Soybeans

1 CUP SOYBEANS OR PINTO BEANS
6 CUPS WATER TO SOAK BEANS
3 CUPS WATER TO COOK BEANS
¼ TEASPOON SEA SALT
1 MEDIUM ONION
½ GREEN PEPPER
1 SMALL CARROT
1 TEASPOON SESAME OIL
2-3 TABLESPOONS MISO
4-5 TABLESPOONS TAHINI

Soak beans 12-18 hours. If the weather is warm, keep them in a cool place or refrigerate to prevent fermentation while soaking. At the end of the soaking time, pour off soaking water, place beans in a pressure cooker, and add fresh water. Bring to pressure, reduce heat to low, and cook 1 hour for pinto beans, 2 hours for soybeans. When pressure comes down, add salt and simmer for 10 minutes.

Preheat oven to 350°F. Dice vegetables and sauté, adding to oiled skillet in the order in which they are listed above. Add miso to vegetables, mix well, and remove skillet from heat. Add tahini. Combine vegetable mixture with soybeans, place in a casserole or baking dish, cover, and bake for 40 minutes. Vegetables should be tender when pierced with a chopstick.

Boiled Watercress and Mustard Greens

1 BUNCH WATERCRESS, WASHED

1 CUP MUSTARD GREENS, WASHED AND COARSELY CHOPPED

1 TEASPOON TAMARI

$^1/_8$ TEASPOON GRATED FRESH GINGER ROOT

Place $^1/_4$ " of water in a pot and bring to a boil. Simmer watercress, stirring constantly to cook evenly, for 45 seconds. Remove and drain watercress, returning the cooking water to the pot. Chop cress into 1" pieces and place in a bowl. Bring cooking water back to a boil and cook mustard greens about 1 minute. Remove and drain greens, again reserving the cooking water. Mix mustard greens with watercress. If cooking water does not taste too bitter, mix 3 tablespoons of it with $^1/_8$ teaspoon grated ginger and 1 teaspoon tamari to make a sauce. If cooking water is too bitter, use plain warm water. Pour the tamari-ginger sauce over the watercress and mustard greens and mix. Place in a serving bowl and sprinkle on some roasted sesame seeds (see Sesame Arepas recipe in Latin American section).

Quick Radish Pickles

4 CUPS DAIKON OR ICICLE RADISH, CUT INTO VERY FINE SLICES

1 CUP SHOYU

2 CUPS WATER

1-2 LEMONS, WASHED AND SLICED, SEEDS REMOVED

Combine all ingredients in a bowl. Place a plate on top, and apply pressure with a brick or rock to keep daikon submerged. Pickles will be ready in 2 hours, and they will keep for 7-10 days if refrigerated. When serving, make sure each person has no more than a few slices, as they are salty.

Fruit Kanten

3 CUPS APPLE JUICE

1 CUP WATER

1/8 TEASPOON SEA SALT

5 TABLESPOONS AGAR FLAKES

1 CUP SLICED FRESH FRUIT IN SEASON (BERRIES, PEACHES, MELON)

Bring juice, water, and salt to a boil in a saucepan. Sprinkle agar flakes over boiling liquid, stirring to dissolve. Lower flame and simmer 5 minutes. Rinse a mold or shallow bowl in cold water and pour in kanten mixture. Let sit until it begins to thicken (about 20 minutes) then add fresh fruit. Mix gently and let sit until jelled (about 2 hours at room temperature).

Variations

■ For a simple meal, serve Mountain Soybeans, plain rice, and Watercress and Mustard Greens. Serve Kanten for dessert.

■ Sukiyaki makes an excellent one-dish meal for informal small parties.

■ Sushi is excellent for picnics and lunchboxes as it is attractive, compact, and keeps well without refrigeration. It is refreshing for summer meals. Double the recipe amounts to have leftovers for the next day.

■ Leftover Sukiyaki is delicious tucked into Pita Bread spread with leftover salad dressing or Hummus (see Middle Eastern Dinner for Pita Bread and Hummus).

C·H·I·N·E·S·E

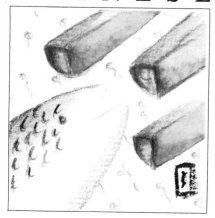

Egg Drop Soup
Spring Rolls with Mustard Dipping Sauce
Red-Simmered Fish
Stir-Fried Vegetables
Sweet and Sour Seitan
Golden Sizzling Rice
Icicle Salad with Hot and Sour Dressing
Almond Cookies

Chop suey, considered by many non-Chinese people to be the definitive Chinese dish, is actually the result of a practical joke. The Viceroy Li Hung Chang was plagued by American newspaper reporters during a trip to Washington, D.C., in the early part of this century. The reporters wanted to know the name of the Chinese dish in which the ingredients were chopped up into little pieces. Frustrated by the absurdity of their question and the rudeness of their insistence, Chang answered the reporters by shouting, "Chop suey!" Literally, his exclamation meant "dirty mixed fragments." However, dauntless restaurateurs all over America overlooked the literal translation and chop suey's place on the American dinner menu was firmly established.

Chop suey and chow mein are hardly representative of traditional styles of cooking in China. The only thing they have in common with the dishes of Chinese peasants is their extensive use of many different fresh vegetables. In fact, most Chinese restaurants prepare food in the Cantonese style, using mostly stir-frying and crispy cooking. Yet this represents only one type of Chinese cooking. Other styles that have developed in China are the Peking style of more elaborate cooking with sauces, Shanghai style using steaming in order to bring out the natural flavors of the ingredients, Szechuan and Yunnan styles which are spicy and chewy. However, even those restaurants which attempt a presentation of these styles are usually quite limited in their repertoire, and provide a very poor representation of the range of Chinese cuisine.

Our meal, including a vegetarian version of "spring rolls" (more commonly known as egg rolls), whole-cooked fish, and a "sweet and sour" dish, utilizes the extensive variety of Chinese cooking styles. It is possible, by selecting among the dishes presented here, to prepare an authentic meal reminiscent of Chinese restaurant food but very close to traditional Chinese cuisine.

Menu (Serves 6-8)

Egg Drop Soup
Spring Rolls with Mustard
  Dipping Sauce
Red-Simmered Fish
Stir-Fried Vegetables
Sweet and Sour Seitan
Golden Sizzling Rice
Icicle Salad with Hot and
  Sour Dressing
Almond Cookies

Cooking Suggestions

■ Most of these dishes are cooked at the last minute, so it is helpful to have all ingredients measured and all the vegetables cut and ready to cook. The dressing for the Icicle Salad can be made the day before (does not need refrigeration if only kept for a day). Raw Spring Rolls keep for about a week if refrigerated.

Egg Drop Soup

1 STRIP KOMBU, 4 INCHES LONG

8 CUPS COLD WATER

1 TEASPOON SEA SALT

4 CUPS MUSTARD GREENS, CUT INTO ½" PIECES

2 EGGS, BEATEN

1-2 TABLESPOONS TAMARI

Bring kombu, water, and salt to a boil. Reduce heat and simmer 10 minutes. Remove kombu and add greens. Turn off flame immediately. Thread beaten eggs into the stock, stirring constantly with a long-handled wooden spoon or with chopsticks. Taste, and adjust seasoning with tamari to taste. Serve immediately.

Spring Rolls   Makes 15

1 ½-2 POUNDS MUNG BEAN SPROUTS

2 CUPS TIGHTLY PACKED WATERCRESS, CUT INTO 2-INCH PIECES

1 TABLESPOON ARROWROOT DILUTED IN 3 TABLESPOONS COLD WATER

15 EGG ROLL WRAPPERS (AVAILABLE AT ORIENTAL OR NATURAL FOODS STORES)

3-4 INCHES SAFFLOWER OR OTHER OIL FOR DEEP FRYING

Blanch vegetables separately, drain, and cool. Squeeze vegetables to remove excess liquid. All ingredients should be as cool and dry as possible. Combine blanched vegetables in a bowl. These will be the filling. Ingredients for alternative fillings are listed on page 42.

Have ready 2 cookie sheets—1 to hold wrapped, raw Spring Rolls and 1 with 3 layers of paper towels to absorb excess oil from frying—and 1 small bowl containing the diluted arrowroot.

Place 1 tablespoon filling near one corner of an egg roll wrapper. Roll corner over filling and tuck point under. Fold sides in. Paint last corner with arrowroot mixture and roll tightly to seal. Place on sheet, sealed side down. Continue till all rolls are ready for frying.

Mustard Dipping Sauce

---

2 TABLESPOONS POWDERED MUSTARD

½ CUP WATER

Mix into a paste in a bowl. Cover with a plate and let stand 10 minutes. Add more water if a thinner sauce is desired. This is very hot!

ALTERNATIVE FILLING INGREDIENTS (Use as few or as many as you like):
- ☐ Shredded cabbage, blanched
- ☐ Broccoli flowerets, blanched
- ☐ Celery, cut thin, blanched
- ☐ Carrots, cut thin, blanched
- ☐ Dried shrimp, soaked 1 hour and cut into small pieces
- ☐ Fresh white fish, cut in small pieces
- ☐ Mushrooms, chopped

As an alternative to Mustard Dip, Spring Rolls can be complemented by shoyu dipping sauce (see Sushi recipe, page 27), sweet and sour sauce (see Sweet and Sour Seitan, page 46), Quick Radish Pickles (see page 34), or slices of lemon or lime.

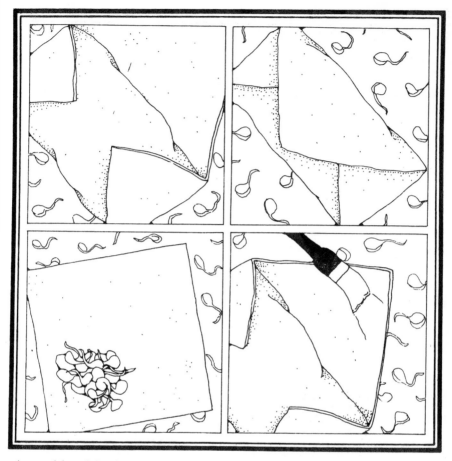

Assembly of Spring Rolls as explained on page 41. Use a modest amount of filling and be careful to wrap the rolls snugly.

Red-Simmered Fish

8 SLICES FRESH GINGER ROOT

6 WHOLE SCALLIONS, CUT IN 2-INCH LENGTHS

2 CUPS RICE OR CIDER VINEGAR

1 ½ CUPS SHOYU

2 CUPS CHOPPED FRESH PINEAPPLE WITH ITS JUICE,
OR 2 CANS UNSWEETENED PINEAPPLE

2 ½ POUNDS WHOLE, CLEANED SMELTS (ABOUT 16)
OR 2 AVERAGE-SIZED MACKEREL, CLEANED AND CUT
IN 1″ CROSSWISE SLICES (LEAVE BONES IN)

Lay ginger and scallions in a saucepan. Cover with vinegar, shoyu, and 1 cup of pineapple, plus juice. Put fish on top. Bring to a boil, reduce heat, and simmer for 2 hours. Remove fish carefully and place it in a shallow dish. Refrigerate. Serve chilled on a bed of greens and garnish with the other cup of pineapple.

Use Red-Simmered Fish as an appetizer or side dish. It will keep for about one week in the refrigerator.

Stir-Fried Vegetables

1 BUNCH (OR HEAD) BOK CHOY

1 ½ POUNDS SNOW PEAS OR SUGAR SNAP PEAS

2 TABLESPOONS SESAME OIL

5 THIN SLICES FRESH GARLIC

½ TEASPOON SEA SALT

2 CUPS SLICED FRESH MUSHROOMS OR CHINESE
STRAW MUSHROOMS

1 CUP KERNELS CUT FROM EARS OF FRESH CORN OR
1 CAN WHOLE BABY CORN, WELL DRAINED

3 TABLESPOONS ARROWROOT POWDER

3 DASHES CHINESE HOT PEPPER OIL

2 TEASPOONS SHOYU

1/3 CUP COLD WATER

Wash bok choy and cut each stalk where the green and white parts meet. Cut the greens into 1″ slices lengthwise and then into 2″ slices crosswise. Cut the white portions in half lengthwise and then into 2″ slices crosswise. The cut greens and whites should measure approximately 4-6 cups.

Blanch peas in a colander by pouring boiling water over them. Heat a wok or skillet for about 30 seconds, then add sesame oil, and when heated, add garlic. Stir-fry garlic until the edges turn brownish, and remove from pan. Stir-fry bok choy whites sprinkled with a little salt. Just when the whites begin to change color and texture, add greens.

Add the peas, then mushrooms and corn and, keeping flame high at all times, heat thoroughly. Combine arrowroot, pepper oil, shoyu, and cold water in a bowl.
 Add mixture to the hot vegetables, turning vegetables with a broad paddle as sauce cooks. As soon as the sauce looks like a glaze, remove from heat and serve. Vegetables should keep their crisp textures and bright colors.

Sweet and Sour Seitan

1. PREPARATION
Tempura Batter

2 CUPS WHOLE WHEAT PASTRY FLOUR
3 TABLESPOONS ARROWROOT POWDER
¼ TEASPOON SEA SALT
1 ½ CUPS WATER

Combine all ingredients for batter and mix until smooth. If you prefer a thinner batter add a little more water and mix again unitl smooth.

Seitan

5 CUPS SEITAN (see page 110) CUT INTO LARGE BITE-SIZED PIECES
OIL FOR DEEP FRYING

Dip seitan pieces in tempura batter and deep-fry in hot oil until golden. Drain on paper toweling and set them aside.

Vegetables

4 CARROTS, SLICED THINLY
6 STALKS CELERY CUT INTO ½ " LENGTHS
3 CUPS SEASONED STOCK FROM MAKING SEITAN (see page 110), OR 2 ½ CUPS WATER WITH ½ CUP SHOYU OR TAMARI

Place vegetables in a pot and add stock to cover them three-quarters of the way. Bring to a boil and simmer, covered, for 15 minutes or until vegetables are tender.

Sweet and Sour Sauce

1 CUP STARCH WATER RESERVED FROM MAKING SEITAN (see page 110) OR 2 TABLESPOONS ARROWROOT POWDER DILUTED IN 1 CUP WATER
1 CUP WATER OR STOCK
½ CUP RICE VINEGAR OR CIDER VINEGAR
¾ CUP BARLEY MALT
½ TEASPOON GRATED GINGER ROOT
2 SCALLIONS, SLICED

Combine all ingredients (except scallions) in a bowl and mix well.

2. ASSEMBLY

Add Sweet and Sour Sauce to vegetables. Simmer, stirring, until sauce thickens. Mix in tempuraed seitan pieces. Transfer to a serving bowl and garnish with scallion slices.

Golden Sizzling Rice

8-10 SCALLIONS, CUT INTO 1 ½" PIECES

3 TABLESPOONS DARK OR LIGHT SESAME OIL

6 CUPS COOKED MEDIUM- OR LONG-GRAIN RICE, COOLED (see page 107)

3 TABLESPOONS SHOYU

3 TABLESPOONS MIRIN (OPTIONAL)

Heat a large skillet over a high flame for 1 minute. Add oil, then scallions, and sauté for 1 minute, stirring constantly. Keeping flame high, add rice and cook for 10-15 minutes. Stir occasionally to prevent scorching but allow the rice to catch on the bottom and become crisp. While continuing to cook, sprinkle mirin over rice and, 2-3 minutes later, add shoyu. The finished rice should be crisp and somewhat sticky, with a deep golden color. Serve immediately.

□ Following are more elaborate variations of Golden Sizzling Rice which can be used in simpler meals or which can accompany less complex side dishes:

SNOW PEAS AND SHRIMP. Blanch snow peas, and soak dried shrimp in water. Sauté shrimp first, then add scallions, rice, and snow peas at the last minute.

VEGETABLE. Cut celery into thin diagonal slices. Place in a colander and pour boiling water over to blanch. Cut broccoli in small flowerets. Blanch almonds or toast in oven. Add celery and broccoli after scallions and rice, just heating them through, taking care not to break them while mixing. Add sliced almonds to garnish.

Icicle Salad

2 PACKAGES SAIFUN NOODLES
8 OUNCES EACH

WATER FOR BOILING AND BLANCHING

2 CUPS OF BROCCOLI FLOWERETS OR SNOW PEAS
OR WATERCRESS

Soak noodles for 10 minutes in 8 cups of warm water. Then boil for 3 minutes. Drain, rinse with cold water, drain again, and cut noodles into 3-inch lengths. Set aside.

Blanch vegetables by placing them in a colander and pouring boiling water over them. Shake colander after each application of water to gently mix the vegetables and expose a new, raw section. Continue this process until all vegetables have been exposed to boiling water. Then quickly shock the vegetables with cold water to stop the cooking action. Drain.

Combine vegetables with cut noodles. Add Hot and Sour Dressing, mix lightly, and serve immediately. Noodles will become mushy if allowed to sit too long before eating.

Hot and Sour Salad Dressing

4 SCALLIONS, CHOPPED FINE
½-¾ TEASPOON SEA SALT OR 1 TABLESPOON UMEBOSHI PASTE
2-3 TABLESPOONS PREPARED MUSTARD
JUICE OF 4 LIMES OR 2 LEMONS

Blend all ingredients until creamy. If a suribachi is used, combine in the following order: scallions, umeboshi, mustard, juice.

Almond Cookies   Approximately 35 cookies

2 ½ CUPS WHOLE WHEAT PASTRY FLOUR (OR 1 ¼ CUPS PASTRY FLOUR AND 1 ¼ CUP RICE FLOUR)
¼ TEASPOON SEA SALT
2 TEASPOONS BAKING POWDER
1 CUP ALMONDS, GROUND INTO 1 ½ CUPS ALMOND MEAL
¼ TEASPOON VANILLA EXTRACT
1 ½ TEASPOONS ALMOND EXTRACT
½ CUP MAPLE SYRUP
½ CUP CORN OIL
WHOLE ALMONDS

1 EGG

2 TABLESPOONS MAPLE SYRUP

Preheat oven to 350° F. Sift flour, salt, and baking powder together and combine with almond meal. In a separate bowl, whip together extracts, syrup, and oil. Add the wet ingredients to the dry and mix well, kneading as necessary to form a heavy, sticky dough that pulls away from the sides of the bowl.

Form dough into balls and press into circles 1 ½" in diameter. Press an almond into the center of each cookie and brush with glaze. Whip egg and 2 tablespoons maple syrup together to make glaze. Bake for 15 minutes at 350° F. Cool before serving.

Variations
■ A simple, one-pot meal can be made by adding more vegetables to Golden Sizzling Rice.
■ Leftover Spring Rolls and, of course, Almond Cookies are welcome additions to the lunchbox.

A·M·E·R·I·C·A·N

Aunt Ruth's "Turkey"
Chunky Mushroom Gravy
Millet "Mashed Potatoes"
New England-Style Baked Beans
Cranberry Sauce
Crunchy Coleslaw
Succotash
Bill's Dills
Mince No-Meat Pie

American cooking is a melting pot of many different nationalities as well as several very distinct styles of regional cooking. Within the various geographic areas of the United States there have evolved ethnic styles of cooking that are quite unique. Such favorites as "cornpone," "hush-puppies," "shoofly pie," "Cape Cod Turkey," "apple pan dowdy," "hoecakes," and "spoon breads" are all "as American as apple pie." In addition, around the holidays of Thanksgiving and Christmas, certain dishes such as turkey and stuffing, mashed potatoes and gravy, cranberry sauce, and pumpkin pie have become traditional. However, they are often prepared with refined sugar and highly saturated fats.

The dinner presented here uses ingredients that are nutritious and wholesome—in dishes that are part of the American tradition. The menu may well evoke memories of many holiday dinners shared with family and friends, but more importantly, we hope, it will be part of a new tradition in your family— the practice of using whole foods.

Menu (Serves 6-8)
Aunt Ruth's "Turkey"
    With Couscous Stuffing
Chunky Mushroom Gravy
Millet "Mashed Potatoes"
New England-Style Baked Beans
Cranberry Sauce
Crunchy Coleslaw
Succotash
Bill's Dills
Mince No-Meat Pie

Cooking Suggestions
■ It is necessary to prepare much of this meal ahead of time. The gluten for Aunt Ruth's "Turkey" must be made at least a day in advance. Cranberry Sauce and the filling for Mince No-Meat Pie become tastier if made a few days ahead. Baked Beans and Coleslaw can be made the day before.

Aunt Ruth's "Turkey"

1. PREPARATION
Wheat Gluten

Render gluten according to the recipe for Seitan in the Appendix, but do not proceed with cooking it in the broth.

Marinade

1 CUP TAMARI

1 CUP SAKE (OR RED WINE AND GARLIC)

1 TABLESPOON GRATED GINGER OR CRUSHED GARLIC

Combine tamari, sake, and ginger or garlic. Knead uncooked gluten in this marinade and let it stand overnight.

Couscous Stuffing

Any favorite stuffing can be used for Aunt Ruth's "Turkey," but couscous has the tendency to become deliciously saturated with the "turkey" juice during baking.

Soak 1 part couscous in 2 parts water for 2 hours. After couscous has absorbed all the water, it can be used plain or mixed with chopped red peppers, parsley, herbs, celery, walnuts, etc.

2. ASSEMBLY
After the gluten has been marinated overnight, prepare the stuffing. Line 3 loaf pans with aluminum foil and then oil them. Separate the marinated gluten into 3 parts. Reserve the marinade for basting while baking the gluten. Roll each piece into an 18″ square, ¼″ thick. Roll quickly and firmly, as the gluten will tend to spring back. Quickly transfer to loaf pans, holding one hand on the bottom of the gluten to maintain shape, while scooping in stuffing with the other hand. Stuffing should fill the loaf, but be loose. Fold one side of gluten over the top and tuck in on the other side. Poke holes and baste with marinade. Bake at 375° F. for about 1 hour, basting occasionally with marinade. Remove from oven when top is brown and crusty and no longer feels sticky (it will look like freshly baked bread). Turn upside down, and let cool slightly. Peel off foil. Slice "turkey" and serve with Chunky Mushroom Gravy.

Chunky Mushroom Gravy

| 2 POUNDS MUSHROOMS |
| 3 MEDIUM ONIONS |
| 1 TABLESPOON SESAME OIL |
| VINEGAR (OPTIONAL) |
| 2 TABLESPOONS ARROWROOT POWDER, DILUTED IN ¼ CUP COLD WATER, OR 1 CUP DENSE STARCH WATER FROM RENDERING GLUTEN |
| TAMARI OR SHOYU |
| SEA SALT |
| PARSLEY |

Cut mushrooms and onions into chunks and sauté in sesame oil just until onions are translucent. Add a dash of vinegar to bring out flavor if you desire. Cover vegetables three-quarters of the way with water. Stir in arrowroot, and season with tamari and salt to taste. Simmer ten minutes. Add chopped parsley just before serving.

Millet "Mashed Potatoes"

| 1 TEASPOON CORN OIL |
| 1 LARGE ONION, MINCED |
| 2 CUPS MILLET |
| 1 HEAD CAULIFLOWER, CUT INTO SMALL PIECES |
| 5 ½ CUPS WATER |
| ½ TEASPOON SALT |

Heat oil in a pressure cooker and sauté onion until translucent. Add millet and stir until it has a sweet, nutty fragrance. Add cauliflower and sauté briefly. Add water and salt, bring up to pressure, reduce flame, and cook for 25 minutes. When pressure comes down, pass mixture through a food mill.

Serve with Chunky Mushroom Gravy.

New England-Style Baked Beans

1 CUP NAVY, GREAT NORTHERN, KIDNEY, TROUT, OR JACOB'S CATTLE BEANS
8 CUPS WATER
1 STRIP KOMBU, 2 INCHES LONG
¼ TEASPOON SEA SALT
2 TEASPOONS FRESHLY GRATED GINGER ROOT
2 TABLESPOONS TAMARI

Soak beans in 5 cups of water for 6 hours. Preheat oven to 250° F. Pour off soaking water, add 3 cups fresh water and the kombu, and simmer over medium flame for 30 minutes. Remove kombu and pour beans with liquid into a beanpot or casserole dish, cover, and bake for 2 ½ hours. Add salt, ginger, and tamari, and bake 45-60 minutes more. Remove pot from oven, uncover, and let sit 20 minutes before serving.

For variation, add a few whole baby onions, chopped carrots, or other hearty vegetables during the last hour of cooking. Place them on top and spoon beans over them just to cover. For baked beans with a sweet taste, add 2 apples, cored and quartered, during the last hour of baking.

Cranberry Sauce

1 ORANGE
1 POUND CRANBERRIES
1 ½ CUPS APPLE JUICE OR CIDER
½ CUP MAPLE SYRUP
2 TABLESPOONS AGAR FLAKES
PINCH SEA SALT

Peel and slice orange and place in a medium-sized bowl. Simmer cranberries in apple juice with salt and syrup for about 30 minutes —about 20 minutes after they pop. Pour hot mixture over orange slices and allow to cool. When sauce has cooled, blend in food mill or blender and return to saucepan. Add agar flakes and cook over low heat for 5 minutes or until agar is dissolved. Pour into a mold. Serve chilled.

Crunchy Coleslaw

½ MEDIUM HEAD CABBAGE, GRATED OR SLICED THIN

½ TEASPOON SEA SALT

WATER TO COVER

4 UMEBOSHI PLUMS, PITTED

½ MEDIUM ONION, CRUSHED OR DICED
(See Directions Below)

3 TABLESPOONS SESAME OR SAFFLOWER OIL

²/₃ CUP COLD WATER

2 TABLESPOONS PARSLEY, FINELY CHOPPED

Sprinkle cabbage lightly with salt. Toss well with hands, squeezing cabbage while mixing. Cover with water and set aside while preparing dressing.

If you use a suribachi, first mash plums, then add onions, crushing them as you mix them in. Mix in oil until it is well blended with plums and onions. Add ²/₃ cup cold water and mix well. If you use a blender, first put in diced onion and umeboshi plums, and then add oil and blend until smooth. Add water little by little while blender is going, and stop when dressing is a uniform consistency. Drain cabbage, squeezing it to remove excess liquid. Add salad dressing and toss lightly. Garnish with parsley sprigs.

Succotash

When succotash was first introduced to the early American settlers by the Indians, it was made with corn and kidney beans. Today it is most often prepared with lima beans.

6 EARS FRESH CORN

6 CUPS WATER

½ TEASPOON SEA SALT

1 ONION

2 TEASPOONS CORN OIL

2 CUPS FRESH LIMA BEANS OR 1 CUP DRY, SOAKED FOR 8 HOURS

1 TEASPOON TAMARI

Cut corn off cob and set aside. Simmer cobs in water and salt for 20 minutes. In the meantime dice onion and sauté in corn oil. After removing cobs from stock, add onion and beans. Simmer 30 minutes. Add corn, season with tamari, and simmer for approximately 10-15 minutes. Do not overcook or the corn will lose its flavor. Transfer succotash to serving dish with a slotted spoon.

Bill's Dills

1 GALLON WATER

½ CUP SEA SALT

4-5 POUNDS SMALL PICKLING CUCUMBERS, OR ONION CHUNKS, CARROT SLICES, AND CAULIFLOWER FLOWERETS

FRESH GARLIC

FRESH OR DRIED DILL

BAY LEAF

Heat the water and salt together to just before boiling. Remove from fire and set aside to cool to room temperature. Wash vegetables. Place vegetables and seasonings in large glass or ceramic containers or pickling crocks. Use about 3 cloves of garlic, cut into chunks, as much fresh dill as desired, and 1 bay leaf per container. Pour in salt water to cover vegetables.

Cover top of each container or crock with a lid or a plate and add just enough weight on top to keep vegetables submerged in salt water. Vegetables which are exposed to air tend to spoil before they can pickle. Let sit 4-6 days.

Mince No-Meat Pie

2 CUPS RAISINS (OR ½ RAISINS, ½ DRIED PRUNES, CURRANTS, OR PEARS)
4 CUPS TART APPLES, PEELED, CORED, AND CUT IN CHUNKS
3 CUPS APPLE JUICE
2 TABLESPOONS RICE OR BARLEY MISO
½ TABLESPOON CINNAMON AND/OR ALLSPICE
½ CUP CHOPPED WALNUTS
2 TABLESPOONS KUZU OR ARROWROOT, DISSOLVED IN 2 TABLESPOONS COOL WATER
1 TEASPOON GRATED ORANGE PEEL
1 TABLESPOON ORANGE JUICE
1 RECIPE PIE CRUST (see page 114)

Soak dried fruit overnight in apple juice.

In a heavy, uncovered pot, cook apples, dried fruit, and apple juice over medium heat for 1 hour. Purée miso with ½ cup of cooking liquid and add to the fruit. Cook for 15 more minutes. Add walnuts and either cinnamon or allspice and mix well.

Add kuzu, orange peel, and orange juice to fruit mixture and cook until kuzu becomes clear (about 3-5 minutes). Let mixture cool while you roll out pie crusts.

Fill pie shell and cover with a full or lattice weave crust. If using a full top, press the edges of the crust together to make a good seal and cut slits to release steam.

Bake at 375° F. for 30 to 40 minutes until crust is brown and firm to the touch. Let cool before serving.

Variations

■ For a light and satisfying meal serve Baked Beans, freshly cooked rice or cornbread, and a salad or lightly steamed greens.

■ For a simple, yet hearty autumn meal, make Millet "Mashed Potatoes" with Chunky Mushroom Gravy, Baked Beans, and Succotash. Serve warm cider for dessert.

■ The filling from the Mince No-Meat Pie is delicious all by itself. Serve it garnished with slices of fresh apple that have been tossed with a little fresh lemon juice to prevent them from turning brown.

■ Fry leftover Millet "Mashed Potatoes" in a little oil with sliced onions for a special Sunday brunch.

■ For lunchboxes, stuff Pita Bread (see Middle Eastern Dinner for recipe) with leftover Aunt Ruth's "Turkey" and leftover Coleslaw.

L·A·T·I·N
A·M·E·R·I·C·A·N

Seviche
Mexicali Rice
Red Chile Marengo
Sesame Arepas
Refried Beans
Corn on the Cob
Marinated Vegetables
Creamy Lemon Pudding

We often associate Latin American cooking with spicy meals. Yet this type of cooking is only done occasionally in the tropical areas of the Americas. The variety of cooking styles in the Latin American countries varies with the geographical terrain and the climatic regions, according to what foods are grown there.

The meal presented here includes many different types of ingredients and cooking styles. All of these are traditional and healthful, revolving around the central grain—corn. Dried flint corn made into corn dough, or masa, is the basis for arepas, tortillas, tostadas, and the many other corn dishes associated with native Latin American cooking. Flint corn, rich in many minerals and vitamins, is more nutritious than sweet corn, and is considered

the staple whole grain throughout Latin America.

Some of the dishes included in this menu give the flavor and feeling of more modern Latin American meals, yet include only whole foods prepared in the most healthful way.

Menu (Serves 4-6)
Seviche
Mexicali Rice
Red Chile Marengo
Sesame Arepas
Refried Beans
Corn on the Cob
Marinated Vegetables
Creamy Lemon Pudding

Cooking Suggestions
■ This is a very convenient meal, as preparation of most of the dishes is done ahead of time. Remember when making Refried Beans that the beans have to soak overnight before first cooking.

Seviche

Seviche, marinated raw fish, is a popular dish in Spanish-speaking countries. The acidity of the lime juice affects the protein in the fish, rendering it "cooked" in texture and appearance.

½ POUND SCALLOPS

½ POUND OTHER WHITE FISH

1 ½ -2 CUPS LIME JUICE, FRESHLY SQUEEZED FROM 1 DOZEN OR MORE LIMES

1 TEASPOON SEA SALT

3 TABLESPOONS PARSLEY, MINCED

3 TABLESPOONS RED BELL PEPPER, MINCED

THIN SLICES BERMUDA ONION

¼ TEASPOON CAYENNE PEPPER

1 CLOVE GARLIC

BOSTON, BIBB, OR RED LEAF LETTUCE

Cut scallops in half if they are large. Slice fish into thin slices with sharp knife. Juice limes and pour 1 cup over fish. Add ½ teaspoon salt. Marinate in a glass bowl 6 hours or overnight. Pour off juice and add new juice, vegetables, cayenne pepper, garlic, and remaining salt. Let sit 2 hours. Arrange lettuce leaves on a platter. Drain fish and serve on lettuce.

Mexicali Rice

3 CUPS MEDIUM GRAIN BROWN RICE
3 ¾ CUPS WATER
½ TEASPOON SEA SALT
3 VERY RIPE TOMATOES, CHOPPED
1 GREEN PEPPER, CHOPPED

Pressure cook all ingredients together, as for regular pressure cooked brown rice (see page 107). Mix lightly to fluff immediately after cooking and turn out into a bowl.

Red Chile Marengo

3 OUNCES DRIED RED CHILES
3 CUPS BOILING WATER
¼ - ½ CUP MISO
8 CLOVES GARLIC
¼ TEASPOON OREGANO
¼ TEASPOON CUMIN POWDER

Break open chiles and remove seeds. Be sure to keep orange seams. Cover with boiling water and soak until soft, at least ½ hour. The water will then be a dark red color. Remove chiles and reserve the water. Purée chiles with garlic in a blender, adding enough soaking water to make paste consistency. Add miso to taste and blend again. Simmer the mixture for 10 minutes.

Use as appetizer dip with chips or raw vegetables or serve Red Chile Marengo as a condiment with the meal.

Red Chile Marengo keeps well in the refrigerator and can be used as a seasoning in stews, soups, and casseroles, as a condiment to accompany beans or tacos, or in a marinade for tofu or fish before grilling.

Sesame Arepas

1. PREPARATION
Basic Corn Dough

4 CUPS WHOLE DRY CORN KERNELS

8 CUPS WATER

1 CUP SIFTED WOOD ASH (HARDWOOD PREFERABLE, CLEAN, NO NEWSPAPER OR TRASH) TIED IN A MUSLIN BAG

Combine all ingredients in a stainless steel or enamel pressure cooker. Bring up to full pressure and cook for 20 minutes. Remove from fire and bring pressure down by running cold water over lid, or let pressure come down by itself. Remove ash bag and drain corn in a colander, being careful to rinse out any remaining wood ash. Return to pot and rinse very well, using 4 or more changes of water and pouring off loosened hulls.

After this pre-cooking, the hulls of the corn should be soft and loose and should float off in the rinse water. (If instead they are still intact or only split but still tough and fibrous, add a little more ash and pressure cook for another 10 minutes. As ash will vary some in degree of alkalinity, so will the amount needed to properly soften the hulls.) After most of the hulls have been rinsed off, return the corn to the cooker, re-cover with fresh water, and continue to pressure cook for 50-60 minutes.

Remove corn from pot and let cool thoroughly. Grind in a Corona hand mill, then knead for 10-15 minutes.

This basic corn dough is used for tortillas as well as arepas, and is the base for many traditional Native American, Mexican, and South American dishes. Corn dough can be stored in the refrigerator but should be used within a week.

Sesame Arepas

2 CUPS SESAME SEEDS

1 ½ POUNDS BASIC CORN DOUGH

¼ TEASPOON SEA SALT

SAUTEED GREEN PEPPERS AND GARLIC (OPTIONAL)

Rinse seeds in a fine mesh strainer, then roast in a dry pan over medium low heat, stirring constantly. The seeds are ready when they are fragrant and crush easily when squeezed between thumb and ring finger. (Forefinger and middle finger naturally are stronger and would exert too much pressure.) Pour seeds into suribachi and place salt into the hot pan for a few seconds to remove any moisture. Grind seeds and salt together until most of the seeds are crushed.

2. ASSEMBLY

Knead ground seeds into the corn dough. For fancy arepas, add sautéed garlic and green pepper at this point. Form the dough into balls, slightly smaller than fist-sized.

Heat a cast-iron skillet that has been brushed with sesame oil. Flatten arepas to 1″ thickness and cook, covered, over low flame for 10 minutes. Turn and cook uncovered for another 15 minutes, till well-seared. Alternatively, you can cook arepas for 5 minutes in a skillet to make them firm, and then bake at 350° F. for 20 minutes or until the surface puffs out.

Refried Beans

2 CUPS DRIED PINTO OR KIDNEY BEANS
1 PIECE KOMBU, 4 INCHES LONG
SESAME OIL FOR SAUTEING
2 LARGE ONIONS, CHOPPED
2 TABLESPOONS CHILI POWDER
2 CLOVES GARLIC, MINCED
2 TEASPOONS CAYENNE (OPTIONAL)

Soak beans overnight in water to cover. Next day, discard soaking water and transfer beans to a pot. Add kombu and fresh water to cover. Bring to a boil and simmer 1-2 hours or until beans are soft. Add water as necessary to keep beans covered. Remove from pot and let sit until cool.

In a large skillet, sauté onions in oil until translucent. Add drained beans, chili powder, garlic, and cayenne. Adding water and turning as necessary, fry until ingredients smell like their flavors have blended, probably about 30 minutes.

Corn on the Cob

In order to make sure that the corn you buy is fresh, check the silk which should be soft and moist, not dry. The husks should be soft, pliable, and green in color, not crisp and yellowing. Few stores or farm stands allow you to strip the ear to check the kernels but you can judge by the feel. The ears should be firm inside the husks. Thin ears that feel soft, surrounded by lots of husk, are immature; the kernels are not fully formed. Large, portly ears are often overmature, and the kernels will be tough. Most farm stands pick their corn in the morning and again toward late afternoon to ensure freshness. Corn on the cob should be eaten the day it is picked if possible; otherwise it loses the bulk of its sweetness.

2 QUARTS WATER

6-8 EARS CORN

Bring water to a boil. Remove husks and drop corn into pot. Bring to a boil again and cook 3-5 minutes. Remove with tongs and serve immediately. Corn can also be steamed in an upright position on a rack in 3 inches of water. Serve with umeboshi instead of butter and salt.

Marinated Vegetables

BROCCOLI FLOWERETS

CARROT SLIVERS

CAULIFLOWER FLOWERETS

ZUCCHINI SLICES

½ CUP LEMON JUICE

¹/₃ CUP OLIVE OIL

1 TEASPOON SEA SALT

Cut up a total of ²/₃ cup mixed vegetables for each person being served. Combine marinade ingredients and shake well in a tightly capped jar. Pour over vegetables and marinate in the refrigerator for 24 hours, stirring often. Serve cool.

Creamy Lemon Pudding

2 CUPS APPLE CIDER
2 CUPS AMESAKE BEVERAGE (see page 114)
4 TABLESPOONS AGAR FLAKES
4 TABLESPOONS ARROWROOT POWDER
¼ CUP BARLEY MALT
2 TEASPOONS VANILLA EXTRACT
4 LEMONS, FRESHLY SQUEEZED
¼ CUP TOASTED, SLIVERED ALMONDS

Place cider, amesake, and agar flakes in a saucepan and stir. Bring to a boil over medium heat and simmer for about 15 minutes, stirring constantly. In a separate bowl, dissolve arrowroot in $1/3$ cup cold cider.

Add barley malt and vanilla to arrowroot and mix thoroughly. Add to saucepan. Let simmer 10 minutes or until thickened. Turn off heat and mix in lemon juice. Chill until set. Garnish with slivered almonds before serving.

Variations:

■ For a light supper, serve only Seviche, Mexicali Rice, and Corn on the Cob.

■ Seviche, arepas, and marinated vegetables are excellent for picnics and lunchboxes.

■ For a delicious "day old" lunch, stuff Pita Bread (see Middle Eastern Dinner for Pita Bread recipe) with leftover Seviche mixed with leftover rice.

M·I·D·D·L·E
E·A·S·T·E·R·N

Celery Boats
Hummus
Pita Bread
Seitan Kebabs
Stuffed Grape Leaves
Cucumber-Chive Salad
Peach Couscous Cake

The Middle East is considered the birthplace of Western civilization. This area of the world is the origin of modern agricultural practices and many foods which have also become popular in other parts of the world. Unfortunately, our modern conception of Middle Eastern cooking is limited to shish-kebabs, baklava, and falafels. These few dishes barely represent the rich and varied cooking of the Middle East, which traditionally uses many healthful foods on a daily basis.

Wheat and barley, the staple grains of the Middle East, are used in a variety of ways as the central dishes in each meal. Couscous, bulgur, and pita bread are among a few of the more common foods that have come to our modern kitchens and restaurants. For the most part, the traditional methods of preparing these foods are still being practiced in the Middle East today, yet most people in this country do not know how nourishing and tasty these foods can be. In addition, the cuisine of the Middle Eastern countries has maintained most of its original charm and quality,

compromising very little with the advent of highly refined and processed foods.

The meal presented here will give you the unique flavor of the Middle Eastern style of cooking. It will allow you to gain an appreciation for the flavor and quality of the ethnic cooking from this part of the world.

Menu (Serves 6-8)
Celery Boats
Hummus
Pita Bread
Seitan Kebabs
Stuffed Grape Leaves
Cucumber-Chive Salad with Tofu
   Mayonnaise
Peach Couscous Cake with Peach
   Sauce

Cooking Suggestions
■ Make the stuffing for the Celery Boats, the Hummus, the Tofu Mayonnaise for Cucumber Salad, and the Couscous Cake a day ahead of time, if desired, and keep refrigerated. Marinate the seitan and vegetables the day before. Pita bread is best made fresh. Stuff the celery, assemble and grill the kebabs, and toss the salad at the last minute.

Celery Boats

1 CAKE SOFT TOFU, 16 OUNCES
1 TABLESPOON UMEBOSHI PASTE
1 TABLESPOON TAHINI
1 CUP BLACK OLIVES, PITTED AND CHOPPED
1 BUNCH CELERY

Boil tofu in water to cover for about 1 minute and drain, retaining cooking water. Blend or mash tofu with umeboshi and tahini until smooth, adding cooking water as needed to make "dip" consistency. Fold in chopped olives. Fill grooves of celery with tofu-olive mixture and cut into 2-inch pieces. The filling tastes even better if you let it sit overnight before using.

Hummus

4 CUPS COOKED CHICK PEAS
2 LARGE GARLIC CLOVES, MINCED
½ CUP TAHINI
½ CUP FRESH SQUEEZED LEMON JUICE
1 TEASPOON SEA SALT
MINT LEAVES FOR GARNISH

Purée first five ingredients in blender, adding water or chick pea cooking water until mixture is thick and smooth. Adjust salt to your taste. Garnish with mint leaves and serve with Pita Bread.

Pita Bread

1 CUP SOURDOUGH STARTER (see page 112)

3 CUPS SPRING WATER

3 CUPS (APPROXIMATELY) WHOLE WHEAT FLOUR
(OR 1½ CUPS WHOLE WHEAT AND 1½ CUPS UNBLEACHED
WHITE FLOUR)

¼ TEASPOON SEA SALT

¼-½ CUP CORN OIL

In a ceramic bowl, make a sponge with starter, water, and enough flour to make a thick batter. Cover with a damp dishtowel and put in a warm, humid place. Let sit at least 8 hours, re-moistening cloth as it dries out, until sponge is "bubbly." At this point, take out a cup of sponge, cover, and refrigerate—this is your starter for next time. Mix sea salt and corn oil into sponge, adding more flour to make a firm, slightly moist dough. Turn out onto floured board and knead for 10 minutes. Place in an oiled bowl, turn dough over once, cover with a damp cotton cloth, and let rise in a warm place for about 1 ½ hours.

Punch down, knead briefly to make smooth, and form into fist-sized balls. Cover and let rest for 15 minutes. Preheat oven to 475° F. Roll out each ball to a thickness of ⅛-¼ inch and place on an ungreased, preheated baking sheet. Place on the lowest oven rack and bake for 10 minutes.

The high heat and quick baking will create a "pocket" perfect for stuffing. While pita is still slightly warm, place in tightly covered storage container to maintain softness.

Seitan Kebabs

1. PREPARATION
Seitan

1-1 ½ POUNDS SEITAN (see page 110)

After boiling or pressure cooking seitan according to the recipe in the Appendix, cut into 1″ cubes and place in a bowl.

Marinade

½ CUP BROWN RICE VINEGAR

1 TEASPOON PREPARED MUSTARD

1 LEMON, JUICED

2 TABLESPOONS TAMARI

5 CUPS WATER

Combine all ingredients. Pour half of this marinade over cubed seitan and toss to coat well. Let sit overnight or for at least 2-3 hours.

Vegetables

1 SMALL SWEET RED PEPPER

1 SMALL GREEN PEPPER

18-20 MEDIUM-SIZED FRESH MUSHROOMS

18-20 SMALL RED RADISHES

Wash vegetables. Slice peppers into 1″ pieces. Separate mushroom stems from caps and set stems aside for use in another dish. Cut each radish in half. Place vegetables in a bowl and add remaining marinade. Mix well and let sit 2-3 hours.

2. ASSEMBLY

To assemble, alternate seitan, peppers, mushrooms, and radishes, beginning and ending with a pepper to keep the vegetables on the skewers. Save marinade, and use it to baste kebabs while they broil. Arrange kebabs on an oiled tray and broil for 10 minutes, basting with marinade. Turn and broil for approximately 10 more minutes, or until vegetables are tender. Serve on the skewers.

Stuffed Grape Leaves

15 GRAPE LEAVES (OR LIGHTLY STEAMED CABBAGE OR COLLARD GREENS)
3 CUPS WATER
1 ½ CUPS CRACKED WHEAT
2 TABLESPOONS TAMARI
½ CUP HULLED SUNFLOWER SEEDS, ROASTED AND CRUSHED
DASH OF BLACK PEPPER (OPTIONAL)
1 TABLESPOON DRIED MINT

Grape leaves, or *dolma,* ready for stuffing can be found at a Middle Eastern grocery or supermarket with a specialty section. Remove grape leaves from jar, rinse, drain, and set aside.

To make the filling, bring 3 cups of water to a boil. Add cracked wheat, tamari, and sunflower seeds. Simmer 3-5 minutes or until water has been absorbed. Turn off heat, add pepper and mint, cover, and let stand for 20 minutes.

Place grape or cabbage leaves vein side down on a cutting board. Spoon 1 tablespoon of filling onto center of each grape leaf (1 ½ tablespoons if you are using cabbage). Fold bottom over once and fold sides in. Roll away from you.

Place stuffed leaves in a baking dish. Add enough water to just cover the bottom of the dish. Cover and bake in a pre-heated 300° F. oven for 20 minutes. Remove to serving platter and garnish with sprigs of watercress or parsley, or with thinly sliced lemon.

Cucumber-Chive Salad

1 LARGE CUCUMBER

2 TABLESPOONS TOFU MAYONNAISE

1 TABLESPOON LEMON JUICE

1 TEASPOON TAMARI

3 TABLESPOONS MINCED CHIVES

Cut cucumber in half lengthwise, then slice across on a diagonal in very thin slices. Combine mayonnaise, lemon juice, and tamari in a small bowl, and mix with a fork. Mix cucumber slices and chives in a glass bowl and gently mix in Tofu Mayonnaise. Let sit at least 10 minutes before serving.

Tofu Mayonnaise

1 CAKE SOFT TOFU, 8 OUNCES

1 CUP WATER

2 TABLESPOONS OLIVE OR SESAME OIL

2 TABLESPOONS BROWN RICE VINEGAR

2 TABLESPOONS FRESH LEMON JUICE

¼ TEASPOON SEA SALT

¼ TEASPOON GROUND CORIANDER

Combine ingredients in a blender and purée until creamy, stopping blender periodically to push contents down with a rubber spatula. Refrigerated, this mayonnaise will keep for 2 days. If the mixture separates, stir well to combine.

Peach Couscous Cake

2 CUPS UNCOOKED COUSCOUS
1 CUP FLAKED, UNSWEETENED COCONUT
4 CUPS AMESAKE BEVERAGE (see page 114)
1 CUP APPLE JUICE
2 TABLESPOONS YINNIE (RICE) SYRUP
1 TEASPOON VANILLA EXTRACT
PINCH SEA SALT
2 CUPS FRESH PEACHES, PITTED AND CHOPPED
½-1 TEASPOON GRATED LEMON RIND

In a large mixing bowl, combine couscous and coconut. Combine amesake, apple juice, rice syrup, vanilla, and salt in a saucepan and bring to a boil. Combine all ingredients, mix well, and turn into 2 oiled loaf pans. Let rest for 15 minutes, then bake for 15 minutes in preheated 300° F. oven. Cool and refrigerate before slicing. Serve with Peach Sauce.

Peach Sauce

2 CUPS SLICED FRESH PEACHES
3 CUPS APPLE JUICE
2 TABLESPOONS ARROWROOT POWDER

Combine peaches and juice in pot and simmer for 45 minutes, or until peaches have lost their form and become very soft. Add arrowroot that has been diluted in ¼ cup cold apple juice. Simmer for 5-7 minutes or until clear and glossy. Chill before serving.

T·R·A·N·S·I·T·I·O·N·A·L

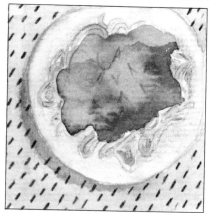

Barley Soup
Lentil Loaf
Ann's Tofu-Broccoli Pie
Sourdough Bread
Millet with Squash
Vegetable Burgers with Gravy
Seitan Stroganoff
Crabmeat Salad
Pesto
Cabbage-Roll Tempeh
Mary's Favorite Tempeh Stew

These recipes are helpful in making the change from a standard Western-style diet to a more natural diet. They are nutritious and balanced, as well as delicious. Reminiscent of many of the foods we have become accustomed to in the West, they will be enjoyed by old and new natural foods enthusiasts alike.

Recipes

Barley Soup
Whole Wheat Sourdough Bread
Crabmeat Salad
Pesto
Lentil Loaf
Ann's Tofu-Broccoli Pie
Open-Faced Vegetable Burgers
   with Mushroom Sauce
Seitan Stroganoff
Millet with Squash
Cabbage-Roll Tempeh
Mary's Favorite Tempeh Stew

Barley Soup   Serves 4-6

1 KOMBU STRIP, 6 INCHES LONG, SOAKED
2-3 MINUTES AND DICED

1 CUP DICED ONIONS

2 DRIED SHIITAKE MUSHROOMS (SOAKED AND SLICED)

½ CUP CELERY, DICED

1 CUP CARROTS, QUARTERED AND SLICED

½ CUP BARLEY, WASHED, AND SOAKED 6-8 HOURS

4-5 CUPS WATER (INCLUDE SOAKING WATER
FROM BARLEY)

SEA SALT, TAMARI, SHOYU, OR DILUTED MISO TO TASTE

TOASTED NORI AND SCALLIONS OR PARSLEY
FOR GARNISH

Place kombu in a pot. Add onions, shiitake, celery, carrots, barley, and water. Cover and bring to a boil. Reduce flame to medium-low and simmer 1 hour, or until barley is soft. Add sea salt, tamari, shoyu, or puréed miso to taste. Simmer 5-7 minutes more. Garnish each bowl with a few pieces of chopped scallion or a little chopped parsley, and several strips of toasted nori.

Whole Wheat Sourdough Bread   Makes 2 loaves

1 RECIPE WHOLE WHEAT SOURDOUGH STARTER (see page 112)
2 CUPS SPRING WATER
5 CUPS STONE GROUND WHOLE WHEAT FLOUR
1 TABLESPOON OIL
1 TEASPOON SEA SALT

Pour starter into bowl and stir in water and 2 ½ cups whole wheat flour. Leave the bowl, uncovered, in a warm place for 1 hour. This "sponge" should be a loose, almost pourable dough.

Return 1 ½ cups of the sponge to your starter jar and refrigerate—this will serve as another batch of starter for use in subsequent sourdough recipes.

Mix the sponge left in the bowl with the remaining 2 ½ cups flour, oil, and salt to form the dough. If necessary, add enough additional flour so that the mixture can be kneaded.

Turn dough onto a floured board and knead until it is smooth and no longer dry or full of cracks. This kneading process takes more time than regular bread dough requires.

Put dough into a lightly oiled bowl, turn it to coat all sides with oil, cover it with a wet cloth, and leave at room temperature overnight.

The following day, punch down dough, knead it well for several minutes, divide it in half, and place into two lightly oiled bread pans.

Let these loaves rise, uncovered, for 2-3 hours in a warm place. When bread has risen to the top of each pan, make a slit 1 inch deep down the length of each with a sharp knife. Place loaves in a cold oven. Set thermostat at 375° F. and bake the loaves for 1 hour or until they sound hollow when tapped.

Turn bread out of pans and cool on a rack for several hours. Loaves can be stored in plastic bags in the refrigerator or wrapped in aluminum foil and frozen for as long as 1 month.

Crabmeat Salad   Serves 4-6

½ POUND FLAKED CRABMEAT, OR FLAKED, STEAMED WHITEFISH (COOLED)

4 TABLESPOONS FRESH DILL, MINCED

4 SCALLIONS, MINCED

1 CUCUMBER

JUICE OF 1 LEMON OR MORE

¼ CUP SLICED WATER CHESTNUTS

½ TEASPOON SEA SALT

Slice cucumber in half lengthwise and scoop out seeds. Dice into ¼″ pieces. Combine all ingredients and mix gently. Serve on individual beds of bibb lettuce accompanied by crackers, or as sandwich filling.

Pesto   Makes 2 ½ cups

2 CUPS SHELLED ALMONDS

¼ CUP OLIVE OIL

5 CLOVES GARLIC

½ TEASPOON SEA SALT

2 CANS ANCHOVIES

WATER TO MAKE A SMOOTH PASTE

4 CUPS FRESH BASIL, WASHED AND CHOPPED

Using a blender, combine almonds, oil, garlic, salt, anchovies, and water. Purée, and when almost smooth begin to add basil. Mix while blending, adding water little by little to make a smooth paste. Serve over noodles— a little goes a long way. Extra pesto can be stored in small containers in the freezer.

Lentil Loaf — Serves 4-6

1 CUP GREEN LENTILS
3 CUPS WATER
1 BAY LEAF
1 TABLESPOON SESAME OR CORN OIL
1/3 CUP CHOPPED ONION
2 CLOVES GARLIC, MINCED
1 TEASPOON EACH OREGANO AND BASIL, CRUSHED
1/2 POUND SOURDOUGH BREAD SOAKED IN WATER FOR 3 MINUTES
1 TABLESPOON FRESHLY GRATED GINGER, OR 1/8 TEASPOON CAYENNE PEPPER
1 TABLESPOON TAMARI
1 TEASPOON SEA SALT
2 TABLESPOONS TAHINI
PARSLEY TO GARNISH

Simmer lentils in water, with bay leaf, for 45 minutes or until soft. Mash with a fork or purée in a blender. Set aside. Heat 1 tablespoon sesame or corn oil in a large skillet. Sauté onion, garlic, and herbs over medium heat for 3-4 minutes or until onions are translucent. Squeeze water from bread and add bread to onion mixture in skillet, stirring well. Add lentil purée to onion-bread mixture. Stir, and continue sautéeing over low heat. Season with ginger, tamari, and sea salt to taste. Cook for 8-10 minutes. Remove from heat and stir in tahini.

Preheat oven to 350° F. Pour lentil mixture into an oiled loaf pan. Bake for 25 minutes or until top is a golden crust. Cool. Run a knife around the edges of the pan, invert, and remove loaf. Garnish with parsley and serve in slices.

Ann's Tofu-Broccoli Pie   Serves 6-8

2 TABLESPOONS TAHINI

3 TABLESPOONS TAMARI

½ TEASPOON SEA SALT

2 POUNDS SOFT TOFU, MASHED

1 TABLESPOON KUZU OR ARROWROOT POWDER

1 POUND BROCCOLI

1 PRE-BAKED PIE SHELL (see page 112)

Combine tamari, tahini, salt, and tofu in a bowl. Dilute kuzu or arrowroot in ¼ cup of water and, in a sauce pan, combine with the first mixture . Simmer over medium-low heat for 7-10 minutes. Wash broccoli, cut into small pieces, and steam until almost tender. Add broccoli to tofu mixture and spoon carefully into baked pie shell. Bake in preheated 300° F. oven for 8-10 minutes to meld flavors. Let cool for 30-60 minutes before serving.

Open-Faced Vegetable Burgers

This is a good way to use up leftovers. Amounts of ingredients are left to your discretion, depending on what you have left over!

COOKED RICE, MILLET, OR OTHER COOKED GRAIN

COOKED CHICK PEAS, LENTILS, OR OTHER COOKED BEANS

TOASTED SUNFLOWER SEEDS

PARSLEY

THYME

SHOYU OR TAMARI

PASTRY AND CORN FLOUR TO BIND BURGERS TOGETHER

If you use chick peas, they should be mashed. Other beans should be of a soft texture. Mix all ingredients together, binding with pastry and corn flours. Pan-fry in sesame oil until brown on both sides. Serve, covered with Mushroom Sauce (see below), as an open-faced sandwich.

Mushroom Sauce

MUSHROOMS
ONIONS
KUZU
WATER

Steam sliced mushrooms and onions. In a saucepan, dilute 1 tablespoon kuzu per cup of cold water for the amount of sauce desired. Add vegetables, and stir over medium flame until kuzu becomes transparent. Add shoyu or diluted miso to taste. Serve burgers with pickles and chips.

Seitan Stroganoff   Serves 6-8

2 MEDIUM ONIONS, DICED
4 CUPS SLICED FRESH MUSHROOMS
¼ TEASPOON SEA SALT
1 TABLESPOON SESAME OIL
4 CUPS SHOYU-SEASONED SEITAN CUT INTO 1″ CHUNKS (see page 110)
1 CUP SEASONED STOCK (from preparing Seitan)
2-3 CUPS WATER
1 POUND SOFT TOFU
½-¾ CUP CONCENTRATED STARCH WATER (reserved from making seitan)
⅓ CUP FRESH PARSLEY, MINCED VERY FINE

Sauté the onions and mushrooms together with salt in a large pot, then add seitan pieces and stock. Bring to a boil, cover, and simmer for 5 minutes. Add water, cover, and simmer for about 20 minutes, or until 10 minutes before serving time. During the time that seitan is simmering, blend tofu and starch water in a blender or suribachi. Add this mixture to seitan and vegetables and simmer for 5-10 minutes. If more salt is needed, use sea salt rather than tamari to keep the color light.

Keep stroganoff mixture warm on a very low heat, as too much heat will cause it to separate and lose the creamy consistency of the sauce. Add parsley just before serving. Serve over fluffy rice or noodles.

Millet with Squash   Serves 6-8

2 CUPS MILLET, WASHED

1 CUP DICED BUTTERNUT OR BUTTERCUP SQUASH, WITH SKIN LEFT ON

1 ½-2 CUPS WATER PER CUP OF MILLET

PINCH OF SEA SALT PER CUP OF MILLET

Place millet and squash in a pressure cooker. Add water and salt. Cover and place on a high flame until pressure comes up. Place flame diffuser under cooker, reduce flame to medium-low, and cook for 15-20 minutes. Remove from flame and allow pressure to come down. Remove cover and place millet in a serving bowl. Garnish with a little chopped parsley.

Cabbage-Roll Tempeh   Makes 4-6 Rolls

4-6 LARGE OUTER LEAVES OF CABBAGE

8 OUNCES TEMPEH

2 ONIONS

1 KOMBU STRIP, 2 INCHES LONG, SOAKED 1 HOUR OR LONGER

Steam cabbage until soft. Cut tempeh into 2-inch rectangles and steam or boil for 15 minutes. Place 1 piece of tempeh in the center of a cabbage leaf and form cabbage roll by folding bottom over once, tucking sides under, and rolling cabbage leaf away from you. Thinly slice onions and soaked kombu. Layer them in the bottom of the pot. Add cabbage rolls and just enough water to cover onions and kombu. Cover, and cook over medium-low heat for 20-25 minutes to reduce liquid by half. Arrange on platter to serve. For a strong dish, first pan-fry tempeh with shoyu. For children, don't add salt, and cook until rolls are very soft.

Mary's Favorite Tempeh Stew   Serves 6-8

1 POUND TEMPEH
$^1/_8$ CUP SESAME OIL FOR FRYING
1 TABLESPOON WHITE MISO, OR LIGHT KOME MISO (OPTIONAL)
1 TABLESPOON PREPARED MUSTARD
¼ CUP SAUERKRAUT
1-2 CUPS WATER
2 TABLESPOONS ARROWROOT POWDER, DISSOLVED IN ¼ CUP WATER TO THICKEN (OPTIONAL)
1 BUNCH BROCCOLI, WITH FLOWERETS WHOLE AND STALKS CUT INTO LARGE MATCHSTICKS
½ POUND CARROTS, SLICED INTO HALF MOONS

Cut tempeh into 8 thin slices: first slice tempeh in quarters, then slice each quarter through the middle. (Thin slices absorb more flavor.) Pan-fry in hot oil until golden.

Combine prepared mustard, sauerkraut, water, and miso (optional) for sauce. Place tempeh in a pot or heavy frying pan and cover with sauce. Cover pot and bring to a boil. Reduce heat and simmer for 15 minutes.

Blanch broccoli and carrots while tempeh cooks.

If desired, thicken tempeh sauce at end of cooking with arrowroot dissolved in water. (Sauce thickens in 1-2 minutes.) Arrange tempeh on platter with blanched broccoli and carrots. Serve with a grain or noodles.

Tempeh cooked this way makes a delicious pocket bread sandwich filling with sprouts.

D·E·S·S·E·R·T·S

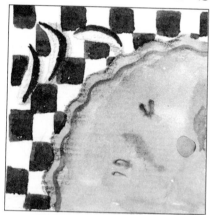

Maple Walnut Cookies
Ron's Delights
Louise's Macaroons
Chestnut-Aduki Brownies
Apple-Walnut Pie
Chestnut Cream Pie
Pecan Pie
Peggy's Squash Strudel
Apple-Raisin Crunch
Fruit Compote with Tofu "Whipped Cream"
Amesake Cream Puffs
Molly's Crêpes

Desserts that are *simply* delicious.

In compiling this section of the cookbook, we came to realize that often the most uncomplicated recipes result in the most delicious desserts! Sweet treats can be as simple and nutritious as they are fun to prepare and heavenly to eat. As the finishing touch to a meal, for a special snack, or to celebrate a special occasion, fresh fruits, grain sweeteners, and whole grains and flours combine to make delightful, extraordinary confections.

Start with fresh ingredients for treats that are wholesome and flavorful. Add your own measure of inspiration to create delectable desserts that your family and friends will ask for again and again.

Recipes
Maple Walnut Cookies
Ron's Delights
Louise's Macaroons
Chestnut-Aduki Brownies
   with Dessert Sauce
Apple-Walnut Pie
Chestnut Cream Pie
Pecan Pie
Peggy's Squash Strudel
Apple-Raisin Crunch
Fruit Compote with
   Tofu "Whipped Cream"
Amesake Cream Puffs
Molly's Crêpes
   with Poppy Seed Filling

Maple Walnut Cookies   Makes 36 2-inch cookies

1 ½ CUPS ROLLED OATS

3 CUPS PASTRY FLOUR

1 TEASPOON SEA SALT

1½ CUPS UNREFINED CORN OIL

1 CUP MAPLE SYRUP

1 ½ CUPS ROASTED, CHOPPED WALNUTS

1 TABLESPOON VANILLA

WATER

Preheat oven to 350° F. Mix oats, flour, and salt in a large bowl. Mix in oil, syrup, vanilla, walnuts, and enough water to make a moist cookie dough consistency. When well mixed, spoon close together onto a lightly oiled cookie sheet, flattening slightly. Bake for 18-20 minutes.

Ron's Delights   Makes approximately 12

These big, delicious cookies were developed by an outdoorsman who likes to take them along on his hiking trips.

4 CUPS WHOLE WHEAT PASTRY FLOUR

1 TABLESPOON CINNAMON

1 TEASPOON DRIED GINGER

1 TEASPOON CLOVES

¼ TEASPOON CORIANDER

½ TEASPOON SEA SALT

¼ CUP INSTANT GRAIN COFFEE

¾ CUP CORN OIL

½ CUP YINNIE (RICE) SYRUP

2 TEASPOONS VANILLA

1 CUP APPLE JUICE OR CIDER

Combine dry ingredients and mix thoroughly or sift. Whisk together all liquid ingredients and add to dry ingredients. Stir until a soft dough is formed. (Adjust liquid content accordingly.) Wrap in waxed paper and chill at least 1 hour.

Roll out to ½" thickness. Cut with 3"-4" cookie cutter or a glass. Place cookies close together on cookie sheet and bake in 375° F. preheated oven 12-18 minutes or until lightly browned and almost firm. Glaze with additional rice syrup immediately after removing from oven. Cool on a rack or brown paper bag.

Louise's Macaroons   Makes 12-16

2½ CUPS SHREDDED UNSWEETENED COCONUT

1/3 CUP WHOLE WHEAT PASTRY FLOUR

¼ TEASPOON SEA SALT

²/₃ CUP MAPLE SYRUP

1 TEASPOON ALMOND EXTRACT

Combine coconut, flour, and salt. Stir in maple syrup and extract. Moistening hand often in a bowl of cold water, form dough into round shapes by firmly squeezing in one palm. Place balls of dough on oiled baking sheet, shape a bit, and bake in preheated 250°F. oven for 30-45 minutes or more until just golden.

Chestnut-Aduki Brownies   Makes 24

1 CUP ADUKI BEANS

1 CUP DRIED CHESTNUTS

3 CUPS APPLE JUICE

¼ TEASPOON SEA SALT

1 CUP PASTRY FLOUR

¹/₃ CUP CHOPPED NUTS

¼ CUP OIL
1 TEASPOON VANILLA EXTRACT
1 ½ CUPS RAISINS, SOAKED IN 3 CUPS WATER FOR 1 HOUR OR UNTIL SOFT, THEN DRAINED

Soak beans in water to cover for 6-8 hours. Roast chestnuts in 375° F. oven for 10-15 minutes, or until fragrant. Pressure cook beans with chestnuts for 45 minutes in apple juice. After pressure comes down, open cooker, add a pinch of salt, and simmer for 5-10 minutes more. Purée bean and chestnut mixture in a blender or suribachi and add remaining ingredients.

Turn batter into an oiled 9″ x 13″ cake pan and bake for 1 hour at 375° F. Serve with Dessert Sauce.

Dessert Sauce

1 CUP RAISINS OR CURRANTS
2 ½ CUPS WATER
1 TABLESPOON KUZU OR ARROWROOT POWDER
½ TEASPOON GRATED ORANGE RIND

Simmer raisins or currants in water with a pinch of salt for 20 minutes. Dilute kuzu or arrowroot in ¼ cup cold water and add to the sauce. Cook for a few minutes more or until sauce has turned clear and begins to thicken. Turn off heat and add grated orange rind. The sauce can be put through a food mill or blender for a smooth consistency.

Apple-Walnut Pie   Serves 6-8

2 POUNDS APPLES (TART APPLES ARE VERY GOOD)
½ CUP APPLE CIDER
1 TEASPOON LEMON JUICE
¼ TEASPOON SEA SALT
¼ TEASPOON CINNAMON

½ CUP ROASTED AND CHOPPED WALNUTS

1 TEASPOON ARROWROOT POWDER

1 RECIPE PIE CRUST (see page 114)

Peel and core apples. Cut them in ¼″ rounds and place them in a mixing bowl with cider, lemon juice, salt, cinnamon, walnuts, and arrowroot. Mix well. Place filling in pie shell and cover either with full or lattice crust. Bake for 30-40 minutes in a preheated 375° F. oven.

Chestnut Cream Pie   Serves 6-8

1 ½ CUPS DRIED CHESTNUTS

6 CUPS WATER FROM SOAKING CHESTNUTS

½ TEASPOON SEA SALT

½ CUP WHOLE OATS

2 CUPS WATER

1 TEASPOON VANILLA

2 TABLESPOONS MAPLE SYRUP (OPTIONAL)

1 PRE-BAKED PIE SHELL (see page 112)

¼ CUP TOASTED ALMONDS

Soak chestnuts in 6 cups of water for 6 hours, then pressure cook in soaking water for 45 minutes. When pressure comes down, add ¼ teaspoon salt and simmer for 10 minutes, uncovered. Dry roast oats in a heavy skillet, stirring constantly, until they impart a sweet smell, similar to that of vanilla. Grind oats into flour. Boil 1 ½ cups water in a heavy saucepan, moisten oat flour with remaining ½ cup water, and stir briskly into the boiling water. Add ¼ teaspoon salt, stir until mixture thickens, cover, and cook over a low flame for 20 minutes. Drain chestnuts and save cooking liquid. Blend chestnuts and oat cream in a blender, adding chestnut cooking liquid as necessary to obtain a smooth consistency. Add vanilla and maple syrup while blending. Pour into baked pie shell and chill. Garnish with slivered, toasted almonds.

Pecan Pie   Serves 6-8

3 CUPS THICK AMESAKE (see page 112)

½ TEASPOON SEA SALT

1 UNCOOKED 9-INCH PIE CRUST (see page 112)

2 CUPS PECANS

1 CUP BARLEY MALT

Mix amesake with salt and spread in pie crust. Lay pecans on top and
pour barley malt evenly over pecans. Place in a 375° F. oven and
bake for 30-40 minutes, or until the pecans just start to brown. Set on
a rack and allow to cool before serving.

Peggy's Squash Strudel   Serves 6-8

1 BUTTERCUP SQUASH OR HOKKAIDO PUMPKIN

1 ONION, SLICED

POPPY SEEDS

CINNAMON (OPTIONAL)

1 ½ CUPS PASTRY FLOUR

¼ TEASPOON SEA SALT

¼ CUP CORN OIL

¼ CUP COLD WATER

¼-½ CUP RAISINS

½ CUP ROASTED CHOPPED WALNUTS

To prepare filling, cut squash in half from top to bottom. Remove
seeds and place onion inside one half of the squash with a little water
for steaming. Oil the outside of the squash (this helps to keep the
flavor in) and replace the other half. Put squash in a pan with a little
water so it can both steam and bake. Bake at 400° F. for 1 hour.
Squash can also be steamed or pressure cooked, but baking produces a
richer flavor and texture. When squash has cooked thoroughly,
remove skin.

Mix flour with salt. Add oil and rub in with hands to pebble consistency. Add cold water and lightly knead into a ball. Refrigerate for

15 minutes. Cut into 2 equal portions. Roll out one portion into a rectangle approximately 9″ x12″ between 2 pieces of waxed paper or on pastry cloth to a thickness of $^1/_8″$. Place rolled-out dough on cookie sheet since moving this strudel dough with the cooked squash in it will be quite difficult. Blend squash and onions completely, mix with raisins and walnuts, and spread mixture ½″ thick to cover rolled-out rectangle of dough leaving 3 inches at both ends uncovered. Sprinkle on poppy seeds and some cinnamon (if desired) at this point. Fold over dough, sealing the plain ends to make strudel. Seal ends with a fork. Repeat this entire procedure with the other portion of dough. Bake 20 minutes at 375° F. Slice and serve.

Apple-Raisin Crunch   Serves 6-8

2 CUPS ROLLED OATS

¼ TEASPOON SEA SALT

1 CUP CHOPPED WALNUTS (OR ANY NUT OR SEED COMBINATION)

$^1/_3$ CUP CORN OIL

½ CUP BARLEY MALT

Mix oats, salt, and nuts together. Add corn oil and mix well. Add barley malt, and mix to coat all ingredients. Spread on cookie sheet. Place in preheated 350° F. oven and bake for 15-20 minutes. Turn frequently, at least every 5 minutes, so crunch does not burn.

6 APPLES

1 CUP RAISINS

½ CUP WATER

¼ TEASPOON SEA SALT

1 ½ TABLESPOONS KUZU OR ARROWROOT, DILUTED IN ¼ CUP COOL WATER

CINNAMON

VANILLA

Wash, core, and slice apples. Place in a pot with raisins, water, and sea salt. Cook for 10-15 minutes over medium heat or until apples and raisins are soft. Reduce heat to low, add diluted kuzu, and simmer for 3-5 minutes or until clear. Cinnamon and vanilla can be added toward the end, if desired.

Remove fruit from pan to serving dish and sprinkle on crunch topping.

To make apple-raisin *crisp,* do not bake the crunch topping. Arrange sliced apples in a baking dish and set aside. On top of stove, cook raisins in 1 cup apple juice with a pinch of salt until they are soft. Thicken with diluted kuzu. Pour raisin sauce over raw apples, sprinkle topping on, and bake at 350° F. for 40 minutes.

Fruit Compote   Serves 6-8

2 CUPS MIXED DRIED FRUIT (PITTED PRUNES, APRICOTS, PEARS, PEACHES, ETC.)

2-3 CUPS WATER

PINCH SEA SALT

Place fruit with salt in a saucepan, cover, and bring to a boil. Lower flame and simmer 45 minutes. Allow to cool before serving topped with Tofu "Whipped Cream."

Tofu "Whipped Cream"

1 POUND SOFT TOFU

½ CUP MAPLE SYRUP

2 TABLESPOONS TAHINI OR ALMOND BUTTER

PINCH SEA SALT

1 CUP APPLE JUICE

1 BAR AGAR, OR 1 ½ TABLESPOONS AGAR FLAKES

2 TEASPOONS VANILLA

Cook tofu by simmering in water to cover for 5-10 minutes. Drain tofu and combine with syrup, tahini, and salt, blending until smooth. While bringing the apple juice to a boil, rinse agar bar in cold water. Squeeze out excess liquid and shred the agar into boiling apple juice. If using agar flakes, sprinkle them over and whisk into the juice. Simmer 4-5 minutes or until agar dissolves, stirring occasionally. Pour agar-apple juice into tofu mixture and blend. Stir in vanilla. Set aside to jell. When the mixture has set, whip again and use immediately on Fruit Compote or other favorite desserts.

Amesake Cream Puffs   Approximately 20, 3″ in diameter

1 RECIPE AMESAKE (see page 114)
1 TABLESPOON AGAR FLAKES
2 TABLESPOONS FRESHLY SQUEEZED LEMON JUICE
1 TEASPOON VANILLA
3 OR 4 ORGANIC EGGS
1 CUP WATER
⅓ CUP CORN OIL
2 TABLESPOONS MAPLE SYRUP
½ CUP WHOLE WHEAT PASTRY FLOUR
½ CUP UNBLEACHED WHITE FLOUR
⅛ TEASPOON SEA SALT

Heat 2 cups amesake to boiling, add agar flakes, and simmer 5 minutes. Mix well with remaining amesake and add lemon and vanilla. Chill while preparing puffs.

Preheat oven to 400° F. Have eggs at room temperature. Place water, oil, and maple syrup in a heavy pan and bring to a low boil. Add flour and salt all at once and stir quickly with a wooden spoon to form a ball in the center of the pan. Remove pan from heat. Add eggs one at a time, beating vigorously after each addition.

The dough is ready to bake when the last egg has been incorporated and dough holds together and no longer looks slippery. It has reached proper consistency when a small quantity will stand erect if scooped up on the end of the spoon. Use the dough immediately.

Drop with a spoon onto a lightly oiled cookie sheet, leaving room between puffs for them to expand when baking. Before baking, lightly sprinkle a few drops of water on the puffs. Bake at 400° F. for 10 minutes. Reduce heat to 350° F. and bake for about 25 minutes longer or until puffs are quite firm to the touch. Cool puffs away from any draft before filling.

Just before serving, cut tops off puffs. Fill with amesake cream and replace tops.

Molly's Crêpes With Poppy Seed Filling   Makes 14-16

1. PREPARATION
Filling

¹/₃ CUP POPPY SEEDS

²/₃ CUP RAISINS

1 CUP APPLE JUICE OR CIDER

½ TEASPOON SEA SALT

1 TEASPOON VANILLA

1 TEASPOON ORANGE RIND

Have poppy seed mixture ready to fill cooked crêpes. To prepare, combine poppy seeds, raisins, apple juice or cider, and ¼ teaspoon sea salt. Cook in an uncovered saucepan for 10 to 15 minutes or until most of the liquid has evaporated. Blend with vanilla and orange rind until creamy, and set aside.

Crêpes

2 CUPS WHOLE WHEAT PASTRY FLOUR

¼ CUP PLUS 1 TABLESPOON CORN OIL

2 ½ CUPS WATER

3 EGGS

Combine all remaining ingredients in a bowl or blender and whisk or blend thoroughly until smooth.

Heat a 9″ skillet over medium heat. Brush a very small amount of oil on the surface, and pour in about ¼ cup of batter, while lifting the pan and swirling it around to distribute the batter evenly over the surface of the pan in a thin layer. After 1-2 minutes the edges of the crêpe should be golden and begin to pull away from the sides of the pan. The top of the crêpe should be almost dry and slightly bubbly. Turn the crêpe over and cook for 1-2 minutes on the other side.

Crêpes may be stacked using a clean lightweight dishtowel between each layer. In this way they may be prepared ahead of time and filled at serving time.

ASSEMBLY

Place 1 tablespoon of filling in center, fold both ends toward the center, overlapping, and fasten with a toothpick.

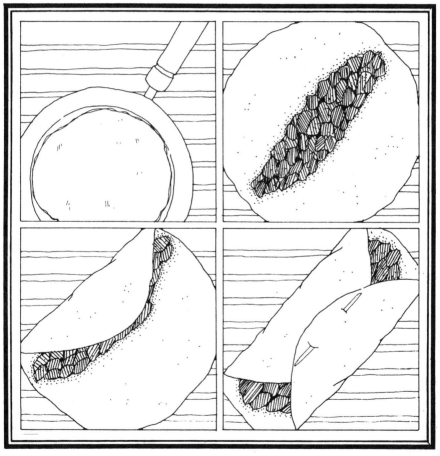

This is the assembly of Molly's Crêpes as explained above. Filling should cover at most ¼ of each crêpe.

Thissectioncontainsinformationaboutseveralbasicfoods,techniques,andfoodpreparationswhichyouwillfindmentionedthroughoutthe*WholeWorldCookbook*.Wehopethatyouwillmasterthesesimple,healthfulrecipesandmethodsandincludetheminyourdailycooking.

Using a Pressure Cooker

The first pressure cooker consisted of an iron pot sunk into the ground on a bed of hot coals. On the pot was placed a tight-fitting lid and on that was placed large rocks to contain the pressure built up in the pot.

Pressure cookers are now often thought of only in conjunction with canning foods. Our mothers and grandmothers used their huge cookers during the harvest but rarely at any other time. Many cooks now, however, find a pressure cooker indispensable for daily cooking— it can be used in myriad ways and sometimes produces tastes and textures not otherwise possible. It cuts the cooking time for beans and whole grains and produces vegetable dishes in minutes. Pressure cooking can therefore allow foods to retain more of their vitamin and mineral content than is possible with other cooking methods.

It takes very little practice to become skilled in using a pressure cooker. Basic directions for operation and maintenance are outlined in the manufacturer's pamphlet that is included with purchase and you should understand them clearly before you begin. However, we'd like to reiterate and emphasize the several most important things to remember:

1. Always make sure the vent (the hole in the cover that the pressure gauge sits on) is clear before you fill the cooker. Make sure the rubber ring is clean and snug-fitting and that all surfaces where the ring and metal come in contact are clean and smooth.

2. Never fill the cooker to more than ⅔ capacity — the food swells as it cooks and might plug the vent.

3. Many foods are not suitable for cooking under pressure— oatmeal, split peas, some dried fruits, etc. They lose their integrity quickly and might plug the vent. Manufacturers will give more extensive lists of these foods in their pamphlets.

4. Never walk away and leave a cooker that is on its way up to pressure at high heat. You will need to be there to turn the heat down immediately when the gauge starts hissing and rocking crazily.

5. While the pressure is up, there should be some intermittent gentle hissing as excess steam is released, and if yours is a cooker with a detachable gauge the gauge will rock gently. If you are cooking on low heat, not enough to produce a constant hissing and rocking, you should check occasionally to make sure contents of the pot are still under pressure. Do this by lightly tapping the pressure gauge. If the pressure is still up a small burst of steam should come out . *Never* lift the gauge to check. If you find that the pressure has gone down altogether, and cooking time is not yet up, turn the heat under the pot up slightly to resume pressure. Don't reheat to high unless cooking time has just commenced.

6. When cooking time is finished, remove the cooker from the heat, or simply turn off the heat under the pot. If you are in a hurry or want to stop the cooking action immediately, carry the cooker, being careful not to tilt it, to the sink and run a small stream of cold water on one edge of the top until the escape valve has gone down. It is better, however, to let the cooker sit until pressure has gone down naturally, and this is the method you should get used to.

The escape valve is your barometer of pressure— it will be pushed up when pressure has accumulated inside the pot and will stay up as long as pressure is maintained. The valve will re-settle when all pressure has dissipated in the cooker. *After* the valve has re-settled, tap the gauge. If no steam or pressure hissing ensues the gauge can be slowly lifted off and the cooker is ready to be opened. If the valve stays in the up position tap it lightly to check— sometimes the moisture will cause it to stick lightly at the up position— if pressure is indeed down the valve will immediately re-settle.

7. *Never* try to remove the cover *until* the escape valve has gone down and the gauge can be lifted off.

So, again, here are the main points to remember in pressure cooking:
1. Clear vent hole.
2. Clean ring and contact surface.
3. Fill to ⅔ capacity only.
4. Some foods should *not* be pressure cooked.
5. Always be there while cooker is coming up to pressure.
6. *Never lift* gauge to check pressure.
7. *Never open* cover until you are sure pressure is completely down.

As intimidating as it looks at first, it will all become second nature to you, however, and you will soon find yourself automatically following these rules without having to think about them. Your pressure cooker will become your best kitchen partner and you'll wonder how you ever got along without one.

Brown Rice

A simple bowl of steaming hot, freshly-cooked brown rice can be most comforting and satisfying when you're hungry. Macrobiotic cooks have discovered a host of delicious variations for serving this staple grain.

Place a measured amount of rice into pot and check through for any small stones. Wash thoroughly by running cold water into the pot, "swishing" the rice around with your hand, then pouring off the water. Repeat 3 or 4 times, or until the water runs off clear. To avoid losing any grains, touch lightly with the back of your hand any that float to the surface—they'll fall back down—or pour through a sieve.

For pressure cooking, measure 1 ¼ to 1 ½ cups water per cup of rice, depending on how sticky or dry you want it to turn out. Add a pinch of sea salt, close the cooker, and heat on medium-low flame. Turn flame up to high after 10 minutes. When pressure is up, place a heat diffuser under the pot, turn flame to medium-low, and allow to cook for 50 minutes. Check pressure gauge occasionally to make sure the flame is high enough to keep pressure up.

Remove from heat and allow pressure to come down before opening. When pressure is down, open pot and, with a wet rice paddle, gently fluff rice by first running the paddle around the side, pulling rice away from side of pot. Pull gently up from the bottom to mix in the "bottom rice." Turn rice out immediately into a wide bowl, allowing it to remain fluffed. Don't pack the rice down—it likes to breathe. Place a bamboo sushi mat on the fresh rice rather than a tight cover.

For boiled rice in hot weather, or if you don't have a pressure cooker, a heavy pot works best. Wash rice as described above, and use 1½-1¾ cups water to 1 cup of rice. Add salt, cover tightly, and bring to a boil over medium flame.
Turn flame to low, place heat diffuser under pot, and allow rice to simmer for 50-60 minutes. When finished, treat boiled rice the same as pressure-cooked.

Some cooks find that washing the rice in the morning and allowing it to soak for 6-8 hours before cooking works well. In this case, add salt only just before cooking, and start immediately on high flame.

Seitan

Wheat gluten, wheat "meat," seitan—by whatever name it goes, this marvelous substance is a welcome addition to whole foods cooking. Through a simple process the gluten in whole wheat flour is separated from the bran and starch, leaving an elastic mass which is then flavored by cooking in a seasoned broth. The resulting meat-like seitan has culinary possibilities limited only by the cook's imagination.

Seitan can be used alone or in combination with grains and/or vegetables, in soups, stews, casseroles, and salads. It can be marinated, pan-fried, deep-fried, and even ground up for burgers. It makes an excellent sandwich with sauerkraut and mustard, and can serve as the base for chili, stroganoff, and spaghetti sauce.

Once you have mastered the simple art of seitan-making, you will sing its praises—and your family and friends will sing yours.

In a large mixing bowl, combine 8 cups whole wheat flour and 6 cups or so of water. (These proportions will yield approximately 2 pounds of seitan.) Mix well and knead this dough in the bowl for 5-7 minutes. It will become very glutinous (sticky) as the gluten develops from kneading. Pat the dough down, cover with water, and let rest for 10-20 minutes.

Begin to knead again in the bowl (under the water) slowly and gently. The water will become milky as the starch begins to separate. Knead a few minutes longer, till the water surrounding the dough is thick and creamy. Pour off some of this "starch water" into a jar, and save it for use in thickening sauces and gravies. You will notice that the heavy, white starch will settle to the bottom of the jar. Pour off and discard the thinner, yellowy liquid and add more starch water from the kneading. Add more water to the bowl as needed and continue to knead. Repeat this process until you have a jarful of thick white starch water. Save only enough starch water as you will use in a week or two. Cover jar and refrigerate.

When you have poured off as much starch as you like, begin pulling and rinsing the dough under gently running water (place bowl directly under the faucet). The bran will now be separating from the gluten and you can, if you desire, devise a way to save it for use in breads and cookies. Otherwise let it run out and down the drain by tilting the bowl occasionally as you rinse.

You should by now have a recognizable mass of gluten—rubbery, elastic, and shiny. Some cooks prefer to leave in a little bran, others prefer to rinse it all out. In any event, by this stage you should have to pull quite hard to work the gluten.

When all but a few specks of bran are left in the gluten and the water surrounding it is running clear, you can call it done (your hands and arms will thank you). This is the gluten-rendering part of the operation. (Stop at this point if you are using the recipe for Aunt Ruth's "Turkey.") Next comes the cooking and seasoning part, which turns the gluten into seitan or "wheat meat."

To season wheat gluten, heat 2-3 quarts of water in a pot with three 4-inch strips of kombu, ½ cup tamari or shoyu, and several large, thin slices of fresh ginger root. Proportions of these can be altered according to your taste. Traditionally, seitan is quite salty.

When the broth is simmering, drop the gluten in. It can be cut into chunks, into 1″ slices, simply pulled apart into manageable pieces, or placed in to cook whole. Alternatively, the gluten can be cooked in a pressure cooker with the same seasonings. It can also be steamed or baked.

When the gluten pieces rise like dumplings they are done. However, longer simmering will cook the flavor into the gluten, making it rich and hearty in flavor and texture. The broth can be totally simmered into the gluten, or some can be rescued and reserved for a stock.

The kombu-tamari-ginger combination is an all-purpose seasoning that creates a seitan that works well in any dish. Try replacing the ginger with onion, bay leaf, and garlic or other herbs for a different flavor.

Occasionally you'll get a batch of flour that just doesn't cooperate— a batch that melts instead of separating neatly. Some say that hard, red winter wheat flour is best, but often you don't know what kind is in the bin at the store. If you do get a "bad" batch of flour, make pancakes instead, and try again with some different flour.

One seitan expert we know uses unbleached white flour—she likes to have starch water available but prefers not to waste the bran, since she doesn't usually include bran in her cooking.

Sourdough Starter   Yields approximately 3 cups

Sourdough starter is a type of home brewed yeast. Instead of using the store-bought yeast that has been developed as a single strain for rising bread, it is possible and enjoyable to develop your own leavening agent from the wild yeast cells living in the air in your kitchen. This traditional technique provides a healthier and much more substantial food.

Yeast, whether sourdough or store-bought, basically works by eating the starch (or sweetener) in the dough and producing alcohol and carbon dioxide as byproducts of its digestion process. The alcohol gives the sour and leavened smell. The carbon dioxide makes the bubbles that cause the bread to rise. Both the carbon dioxide and the alcohol are driven off by the baking.

2 CUPS STONE-GROUND WHOLE WHEAT FLOUR

2 CUPS SPRING WATER

Place flour and water in a glass or ceramic bowl and stir with a wooden spoon to form a porridge-like mixture. It should make a very thick, yet pourable, batter. If necessary, add more flour and/or water to produce this consistency.

Scrape down the sides of the bowl and cover with a sushi mat to protect the contents from dust. Let the bowl sit at room temperature for 2-5 days, stirring daily with a wooden spoon. The mixture is ready when it smells slightly sour. The time depends on air temperature and humidity in the room. In summer it might take only 2 days; in winter it could take several days longer. Stir any liquid that forms on top back into the starter.

Transfer the starter mixture to a small crock or jar. Leave uncovered at room temperature for another day or two until a sweet flavor develops. During this time skim off any dark or gray liquid that might form on top. Cover and store starter in the refrigerator until you are ready to make sourdough bread, pancakes, muffins, etc.

Use your starter according to the sourdough recipe you are working with. In general, re-fill your starter jar from the sponge, if the sponge method is used in the recipe. If you are using a recipe that does not call for a sponge, replenish the starter with dough after the first rising. With a little care and regular use your starter can be kept going indefinitely. The early European settlers in this country carried their precious generations-old starters across the Atlantic Ocean and then across the continent.

Amesake   Yields 5 cups thick amesake or 10 cups beverage

This special dessert food gets its sweetness from glutinous sweet brown rice in combination with the fermenting action of the koji bacillus, which also makes it highly digestible.

1 ½ CUPS SWEET RICE
3 ½ CUPS WATER
½ CUP KOJI RICE (Available at Oriental groceries and natural foods stores)
PINCH SEA SALT

Wash sweet rice and pressure cook with water for 1 hour. Remove to a ceramic bowl and cool for 15-20 minutes, stirring occasionally. Add koji rice and mix well. Cover with a sushi mat and let sit for 8-10 hours, stirring occasionally. The length of time it takes for this fermented food to develop its maximum sweetness will depend on the temperature of the air surrounding it. In winter it will take longer, but be careful not to let it go past sweet and turn to sour. (If the mixture does turn sour, add enough corn flour and whole wheat flour to make a very thick batter, and bake for a delicious cake-like bread.)

When the rice mixture has become very sweet, return to the pot, add a pinch of salt and simmer for 20-30 minutes to stop the fermenting action. This is "thick" amesake, with the consistency of porridge. Cool, and store in the refrigerator.

For a refreshing beverage, add 4-5 cups more water before cooking. Blend very well in a blender before storing. This beverage can be used in most dessert recipes that call for sweet liquid.

All Purpose Pie Crust   Yields 1 full crust or 2 bottom crusts

Whole wheat pastry flour makes a very tender crust but can be difficult to work with because it lacks gluten. Use some unbleached white flour with the pastry flour to make a dough that is more pliable. Other combinations of flours can be used as well, such as whole wheat, corn and oat. Experiment with combinations and proportions to create your own favorites.

The following proportions yield a versatile pie crust, suitable for use with a variety of fillings.

---

3 CUPS WHOLE WHEAT PASTRY FLOUR (OR 1 ½ CUPS PASTRY AND 1 ½ CUPS UNBLEACHED WHITE)

½ TEASPOON SEA SALT

½ CUP CORN OIL

½ CUP COLD WATER OR JUST ENOUGH TO MAKE A WORKABLE DOUGH

Combine flour and salt in a mixing bowl. Add oil all at once and work into flour lightly and deftly with a fork until the oil coats the flour. The mixture should have a pebbly consistency. Add water all at once, mixing quickly with a fork until a ball of dough is formed in the center of the bowl. Roll out half of the dough on a lightly floured board (or between 2 pieces of waxed paper, wetting the surface under the bottom paper to prevent sliding). Use light, short strokes, working out from center. When dough is half rolled out, use longer strokes, applying more pressure. This ensures an even crust. Peel off top piece of paper and invert rolled dough into 9″ pie pan. Peel off bottom layer of paper. If rolling on floured surface, turn dough over when half rolled out, lightly re-flouring surface, before proceeding. When finished rolling, fold dough carefully in half to place onto pie plate.

Roll out top crust similarly. Fill pie. Invert top crust to cover, or cover with a lattice weave. If you prepare a full top crust, trim excess with a knife and flute the edges by holding the edge of the crust with the thumb and forefinger of one hand and pushing between them, toward the center of the pie, with the forefinger of your other hand. Be sure to cut slits in the top crust before baking to allow steam to escape.

If using a recipe that calls for a pre-baked pie shell, bake the shell at 375° F. for 10-12 minutes. To prevent pre-baked shells from bubbling, prick them with a fork or sprinkle one-half cup of dry beans in the bottom of the shell before baking. Remove beans when pre-baked shell is cool.

In general, bake filled pies at 350° F. for approximately 35-40 minutes, or until the crust is golden.

Pasta

A distinction is made by the United States Food and Drug Administration between pasta and noodles. Noodles by definition must contain eggs; if not, the product must be called pasta. Oriental imports are the exception to this rule; they can be legally classified as noodles even if they do not contain eggs. Macrobiotic cooking rarely employs eggs. For the sake of convenience, the word "pasta" will be used in the following discussion, though Oriental "noodles" are prepared in the same way. Either of these are appropriate for the following recipe.

There are general rules for cooking pasta. Use a thin pot with high sides. Use 10 cups of water for 1 pound of pasta. Bring water to a boil over a high flame and add salt if there is none in the pasta. Add pasta all at once. When the water boils again, add 1 cup of cold water; bring to a boil two more times, each time adding 1 cup of cold water (this method is called "shocking"). When the water comes to a boil the fourth time, taste the pasta: it should be perfectly done. Thin Oriental soup noodles need to be shocked only twice with water.

If cooked pasta will be allowed to sit before use, it should be rinsed immediately after cooking under cold water to prevent further cooking. Even if you are adding the pasta immediately to vegetables or soup, you still need to rinse it to remove the surface starch that forms during cooking.

One exception to this method of cooking is whole wheat pasta. To cook 1 pound of whole wheat pasta, first boil 12 cups water, and then add salt and pasta. Cook approximately 10 minutes (depending on the texture of the pasta), then turn off flame and let sit 4-5 minutes. Drain in a colander and rinse thoroughly under cool water. This method allows the bran in the wheat to soften, and prevents the pasta from overcooking.

Pasta absorbs flavors quickly. If you prepare a dish and must let it sit awhile before serving, compensate by adding a little more salt to the pasta as it cooks and season with strong herbs such as garlic, scallions, and basil. Just before adding it to your dish, rinse pasta briefly under hot water and drain thoroughly, shaking off excess water.

Agar. A white gelatin derived from a sea vegetable used in making kanten and aspics. Kanten is excellent in the summer as a cool, refreshing dessert.

Amesake. A sweetener or refreshing drink made from sweet rice and koji starter that is allowed to ferment into a thick liquid. Hot amasake is a delicious sweet beverage on cold autumn or winter nights.

Arame. A thin, wiry black sea vegetable similar to hiziki, often used as a side dish. Arame is rich in iron, calcium, and other minerals.

Arrowroot Powder. A starch flour processed from the root of an American native plant. It is used as a thickening agent, similar to cornstarch or kuzu, in making sauces, stews, gravies, or desserts.

Barley Malt. A thick, dark brown sweetener made from barley or a combination of barley and corn. Used in making desserts, sweet and sour sauces, and in a variety of medicinal drinks.

Burdock. A wild, hardy plant that grows throughout the United States. The long, dark root is highly valued in macrobiotic cooking for its strengthening qualities. The Japanese name is "gobo."

Couscous. A traditional North African grain made from semi-refined wheat.

Grain Coffee. A non-caffeine coffee substitute made from roasted grains, beans, and roots. Ingredients are combined in different ways to create a variety of flavors. Used like instant coffee.

Kanten. A jelled dessert made from agar. It can include melon, apples, berries, peaches, pears, amesake, azuki beans, or other items. Usually served chilled, it is a cool, refreshing alternative to conventional gelatin.

Kombu. A wide, thick, dark green sea vegetable that grows in deep ocean water. Used in making soup stocks, condiments, and candy, and often cooked with vegetables and beans. Kombu is rich in essential minerals.

Kuzu. A white starch made from the root of the wild kuzu plant. In this country, the plant is called "kudzu." Used in making soups, sauces, gravies, desserts, and for medicinal purposes.

Mirin. A wine made from whole grain sweet rice. Used occasionally as a seasoning in vegetable or sea vegetable dishes.

Miso. A fermented grain or bean paste made from ingredients such as soybeans, barley, and rice. There are many varieties of miso now available. Barley (mugi) or soybean (hatcho) miso is usually recommended for daily use. Miso is high in protein and Vitamin B$_{12}$.

It is especially good for the circulatory and digestive organs.

Nori. Thin sheets of dried sea vegetable that are black or dark purple when dried. Nori is often roasted over a flame until green. It is used as a garnish, wrapped around rice in making sushi, or cooked with tamari as a condiment. Rich in Vitamin A and protein, nori also contains calcium, iron, Vitamins B_1, B_2, C and D.

Rice Vinegar. A mild vinegar made from whole brown rice or white rice.

Saifun. Chinese transparent "bean thread" noodles.

Sake. A traditional alcoholic beverage made from fermented rice.

Seitan. Wheat gluten cooked in seasoned broth, usually tamari, kombu, and water. Seitan can be made at home or purchased ready-made at many natural food stores. Many people use it as a meat substitute.

Shiitake. A mushroom, often imported dried from Japan, but also available fresh in some stores. Used in soup stocks, vegetable dishes, and medicinally. Shiitake is effective in helping the body neutralize the effects of excessive salt or animal fat consumption.

Shoyu. Soy sauce made from soybeans, wheat, salt, water, and a special starter called koji. It is a very tasty and nutritious seasoning.

Suribachi. A special serrated, glazed clay bowl. Used with a pestle, called a surikogi, for grinding and puréeing foods. An essential item in a macrobiotic kitchen, electric blenders are not recommended for regular use.

Sweet Brown Rice. A sweeter-tasting, more glutinous variety of rice. Sweet brown rice is often used in cooking for festive occasions.

Tahini. A smooth paste made from ground white sesame seeds.

Tamari. The name given to traditional, naturally made soy sauce to distinguish it from commercial, chemically processed varieties. Original tamari is the liquid poured off during the process of making hatcho miso. The best-quality tamari soy sauce is naturally fermented over two summers and is made from round soybeans and sea salt that is not highly refined.

Tempeh. A food made from split soybeans, water, and a special bacteria, that is allowed to ferment for several hours. Tempeh is eaten in Indonesia and Ceylon as a staple food. It is available, prepacked and ready to prepare, in some natural foods stores. Rich in Vitamin B_{12} and protein.

Tofu. Soybean curd, made from soybeans and nigari (a coagulant taken from salt water). Used in soups, vegetable dishes, dressings, etc., tofu is high in protein.

Udon. Japanese noodles made from wheat, whole wheat, or whole wheat and unbleached white flour. Udon generally have a lighter flavor than soba (buckwheat) noodles.

Umeboshi Paste/Plums. Salty, pickled plums. Umeboshi plums stimulate the appetite and digestion and aid in maintaining an alkaline blood quality. Shiso leaves are usually added to the plums during pickling to impart a reddish color and natural flavoring.

Wasabi. A light green Japanese dried horseradish powder that is traditionally used in sushi or with raw fish (sashimi). When prepared it has a very strong, pungent flavor.

Yinnie (Rice) Syrup. A sweet, thick syrup made from brown rice and barley that is used in dessert cooking. This complex carbohydrate sweetener is preferable to simple sugars such as honey, maple syrup, and molasses.

It is possible that some of the ingredients listed in this cookbook will be difficult to locate in your local natural foods store. If that is the case, you may be interested in contacting the following companies, all of which supply packaged high quality natural foods by mail order.

Chico-San, Inc.
P.O. Box 810, Dept. EW
Chico, CA 95927
(916) 891-6271

Eden Foods, Inc.
Mail Order, Dept. E
701 Tecumseh Rd.
Clinton, MI 49236
(517) 456-7424

Erewhon Natural Foods
236 Washington Street, Dept. EW
Brookline, MA 02146
(617) 738-4516

Granum
Dept. J
P.O. Box 14057
Seattle, WA 98114
(206) 323-0892

Mountain Ark Trading Company
120 S. East Street
Dept. EW
Fayetteville, AR 72701
(501) 442-7191

Oak Feed Store
3030 Grand Avenue
Dept. EW
Coconut Grove, FL 33133
(305) 448-7595

East West Journal, one of the nation's principal magazines advocating the importance of a healthful diet, has been published for fourteen years from Brookline, Massachusetts. Long before it became fashionable to dine on granola, yoghurt, and tofu, *East West Journal* was stressing the value of eating less saturated fats and more fiber and complex carbohydrates. The value of eating whole and natural foods is one of the primary topics of every issue of *EWJ.*

This magazine will show you how to eat better and live longer and more healthfully—but you may have to cut your food bill in half to do so. We'll show you how to do it the way the U.S. Government's Dietary Guidelines recently recommended: With whole grains and fiber and a healthful alternative to the standard American diet.

East West Journal is a magazine with an objective: The holistic quality of life...physical, spiritual, and intellectual.

The writers of the *Journal* are people you can trust and rely on. They are people who have made a natural lifestyle their lifestyle. And they write on everything from organic gardening, wilderness trekking, and long distance running, to spinning yarn, making your own pickles, and raising children naturally.

The issue of diet is always part of *East West Journal.* But it's only one part. Each issue of *EWJ* is as eclectic as the holistic view we take of the world. You'll find regular columns on natural healing, ecology, alternative energy, family health, books, and natural foods cooking.

EWJ is available in selected natural foods stores and bookstores throughout the U.S. and Europe. Subscriptions are available for only $18.00 for one year. Please address your subscription order to *East West Journal* P.O. Box 1200, Department W, 17 Station Street, Brookline, Massachusetts 02147.